GUY TALK GIRL TALK

10 GENDER SPECIFIC LESSONS ON EVERYDAY ISSUES YOUR TEENS FACE

small group curriculum

Thank you for purchasing this curriculum from the Better Together line of Small Group resources from Simply Youth Ministry.

Small Groups are a vital part of growing spiritually and remaining spiritually healthy. We're weren't created to do life alone, but rather, together, as a community of believers striving to be more like Jesus. Proverbs 27:17 tells us, "As iron sharpens iron, so a friend sharpens a friend" (NLT).

We need each other! Not just for our need for companionship, but for our need to grow as people and as followers of Jesus Christ.

The Better Together line of small group curriculums from Simply Youth Ministry are designed to help meet these needs. Here are a few features of the Better Together line that you'll find helpful:

Easy to Use
Created with a "just add water" process, these curriculums are very easy to use from a leader's perspective. Whether they're praying for red lights on the way to their small group to prep the lesson, or they've put in several hours of prep time, the lesson structure and content is designed for leaders to effectively teach the material.

Reproducible
Each curriculum comes with permission to make as many copies you need for both the leaders and students within your ministry.

Editable
Customize the material to make it completely relevant to students in your ministry.

Saves Time
You'll never have to question the quality of the material. These curriculums are created by youth pastors in the trenches and sent through a rigorous editing process, so you can trust the material that you receive. In turn, since you don't have to develop the material, you can spend more times loving leaders and pouring into students.

BeTTeR:TOGeTHeR
small **group** curriculum

Fellowship
The Better Together line of small group curriculums is designed to create community through its discussion based nature.

Discipleship
All of the curriculum is Bible-based and designed to encourage students to grow in their relationship with Jesus.

Thanks for making Better Together and Simply Youth Ministry a part of your journey. After all, we're better together!

TABLE OF CONTENTS

TABLE OF CONTENTS

✕ GUY TALK ✕

WHAT DOES IT TAKE TO BE A MAN?

PRIMARY SCRIPTURES
Exodus 4:14,
Ephesians 5:25-31,
1 Timothy 5:8

OBJECTIVES

- Define the biblical perspective of masculinity.
- Take the first steps in being the men God has called us to be.

OVERVIEW

Pick up a men's magazine and you'll find tips on how to get that six pack, the perfect shave, the coolest new gadget, and how to get a woman to sleep with you. And as appealing as these things are, none of them point to what it truly means to be a man. In fact, these magazines actually lead you away from true manhood because they paint a picture of a man who is weak, self-centered and fake.

The Bible shows us qualities of being masculine that our culture doesn't appreciate. It tells us that men are risk takers, adventurers, concerned with purity, passionate, strong, and gentle. It tells us that we are more than just animals who move from one lust-filled moment to the next. We are to be leaders and providers of wellness and growth in our own lives, our families and community.

LEADER'S STUDY

Some people believe their gender is a mistake. Some want everyone to believe there aren't any significant differences among the genders. And because we are exposed to so much pop-psychology through books, magazines, infomercials, and television and radio talk shows, we can begin to develop an assortment of distorted views on true manhood and womanhood.

So how does God define what it takes to be a man? This lesson will reveal three iconic figures from the Bible that we can develop in our lives.

1. The Warrior

The warrior is driven, adventurous and a risk taker, three traits most guys naturally desire. But nothing reveals the warrior in a man better than when he is called to be a protector. Ask any father what he would do to protect his children or wife, and you will see a fire in his eyes that's inspiring. When men protect, they model God:

Exodus 4:14 says: *The LORD will fight for you; you need only to be still.*

Psalm 116:6 says: *GOD takes the side of the helpless, when I was at the end of my rope, he saved me (MSG).*

Guys instinctively desire to protect—whether it's protecting their family, their reputation, their country, or themselves.

2. The Shepherd

The shepherd is gentle, caring and supportive. Guys live this out through their strong desire to provide for their families and communities. This is the motivation that gets a man out of bed early in the morning for work while still getting home in time to videotape his child's soccer game that evening.

Jesus said: *"Look at the birds of the air; they do not sow or reap or store away in barns, and yet your heavenly Father feeds them. Are you not much more valuable than they? Who of you by worrying can add a single hour to his life"* (Matthew 6:26-27).

1 Timothy 5:8: *If anyone does not provide for his relatives, and especially for his immediate family, he has denied the faith and is worse than an unbeliever (NIV).*

3. The Lover

The lover is passionate, faithful and selfless. This element of manhood allows for his sexuality, but keep in mind it is within the context of being faithful and selfless to one woman in marriage. This is also the part of a man that is vulnerable and therefore the most attacked and skewed by the world, culture and media. It is also the role that God's selfless and unconditional love for humanity is most frequently revealed in the Bible. Look at the following verses that describe Christ's sacrificial love for us that challenges men to love their wives in the same way:

Ephesians 5:25-31: *Husbands, love your wives, just as Christ loved the church and gave himself up for her to make her holy, cleansing her by the washing with water through the word, and to present her to himself as a radiant church, without stain or wrinkle or any other blemish, but holy and blameless. In this same way, husbands ought to love their wives as their own bodies. He who loves his wife loves himself. After all, no one ever hated his own body, but he feeds and cares for it, just as Christ does the church— for we are members of his body. For this reason a man will leave his father and mother and be united to his wife, and the two will become one flesh.*

ADDITIONAL RESOURCES (OPTIONAL)

Magazine Survey – Go to a local bookstore and purchase some magazines for men. Go through and remove any photos, headlines, or articles that may be stumbling blocks for your guys. Once you've "cleaned" the magazines up, hand out one or more magazines to each guy in the group. Ask each group to flip through the magazines and find pictures, articles, headlines, or ads that attempt to define what it means to be a man, whether appropriately or inappropriately. Have each group share what they found and to comment on their selections.

DISCUSSION GUIDE

Open Up

- What do you think it takes to be a man?

- Who is someone you consider to be the perfect man? Explain.

- What stands out to you from the following quote:

TIP:
Talk about a recent or memorable adventure.

"Adventure, with all its requisite danger and wildness, is a deeply spiritual longing written into the soul of a man. The masculine heart needs a place where nothing is prefabricated, modular, nonfat, zip lock, franchised, on-line, microwavable. Where there are no deadlines, cell phones, or committee meetings. Where there is room for the soul."
– John Eldredge, *Wild at Heart*

Dig In

Transition into your study by describing how easy it is to allow other people, culture and the media to determine what it means to be a man. The problem with those sources is that they are skewed and twisted; so we need to look to the Bible to see what the One who created us says on the subject. Understanding the biblical standard on manhood is challenging, however, because our culture offers a more convenient and self-centered view. God's plan is more defined but also more beneficial and productive.

TIP:
Each guy may feel a stronger draw to one of the figures, and that's OK. It's a good reminder of diversity in God's design.

Read and discuss the Warrior, the Shepherd and the Lover.

- If someone were attacking a person you care for, your mother or a girlfriend for example, what would you do?

- Describe a time when you experienced the desire to step in and protect someone?

- What opportunities exist today that give teenage guys the opportunity to provide for others? (pay for meals on a date, provide encouragement to a teammate, help a neighbor, etc.)

- What would a typical guy say his priorities were in a relationship with a girlfriend?

- Do those priorities match up with the way Christ says we are to love that person in our lives? Why or why not?

CLOSE OUT

- What changes would most Christian guys need to make to start becoming the man God has called them to be?

- Looking at the three icons—Warrior, Shepherd, Lover—which do you want to further develop in your life? Why?

- How does the Bible's view on what it means to be a man challenge you?

- What is something you can do this week to start becoming the man God wants you to be?

WALKING WITH CONFIDENCE

PRIMARY SCRIPTURE

Jeremiah 29:11-13,
Luke 15,
John 15:15

OBJECTIVES

- Identify what influences our self-image.
- Find Bible verses that reveal our identity as children of God.
- Understand and appreciate the value and worth God gives us.

OVERVIEW

Psalm 8:3-8 says: *When I consider your heavens, the work of your fingers, the moon and the stars, which you have set in place, what is man that you are mindful of him, the son of man that you care for him? You made him a little lower than the heavenly beings and crowned him with glory and honor. You made him ruler over the works of your hands; you put everything under his feet: all flocks and herds, and the beasts of the field, the birds of the air, and the fish of the sea, all that swim the paths of the seas.*

A man's greatest needs are to have worth and be valued. Guys are willing to pursue this at all costs, but we live in a culture that wants to destroy a man's worth and value, so the challenge is to find these in appropriate ways. Solomon, a man the Bible describes as the wisest ever, looked to find worth and value in a lot of different places and in a lot of different relationships. Read Ecclesiastes 2:3-11 aloud to see how that worked out for him.

I tried cheering myself with wine, and embracing folly—my mind still guiding me with wisdom. I

TIP:
This sounds like so many men in our culture, doesn't it? It might even describe the dads of the guys in your group.

wanted to see what was worthwhile for men to do under heaven during the few days of their lives. I undertook great projects: I built houses for myself and planted vineyards. I made gardens and parks and planted all kinds of fruit trees in them. I made reservoirs to water groves of flourishing trees. I bought male and female slaves and had other slaves who were born in my house. I also owned more herds and flocks than anyone in Jerusalem before me. I amassed silver and gold for myself, and the treasure of kings and provinces. I acquired men and women singers, and a harem as well—the delights of the heart of man. I became greater by far than anyone in Jerusalem before me. In all this my wisdom stayed with me. I denied myself nothing my eyes desired; I refused my heart no pleasure. My heart took delight in all my work, and this was the reward for all my labor. Yet when I surveyed all that my hands had done and what I had toiled to achieve, everything was meaningless, a chasing after the wind; nothing was gained under the sun.

Finding worth and value in people and things brings some satisfaction, but just like Solomon found out, it doesn't last very long. Nor does it truly provide satisfaction. We need permanent solutions.

LEADER'S STUDY

Teenagers need to understand what God says about them. They need to know that regardless of how others classify them, God's view of them never changes. Pray for the young men in your group that they would believe the following five truths God declares about them.

TIP:
If you're a dad, share what it was like the first time you laid eyes on your son or daughter. If you're not a dad, interview one beforehand and share his story with your group.

1. "You are My son."

To all who received him, to those who believed in his name, he gave the right to become children of God (John 1:12).

2. "You are My friend."

Jesus said: "I'm no longer calling you servants because servants don't understand what their master is thinking and planning. No, I've named you friends because I've let you in on everything I've heard from the Father" (John 15:15).

What does having a friend mean to you? What is the difference between people you know and people who are your friends? God calls you friend. What does it mean to you that God calls you His friend?

3. "You are worth so much to Me."

Jesus was criticized for associating with people whom the culture didn't value very much. Jesus told three stories to give His critics an idea of just how valuable every person is. They are found in Luke 15—the parable of the lost sheep, the lost coin, and the prodigal son. Read one or all three.

4. "I will always love you."

The apostle Paul wrote: *I am convinced that neither death nor life, neither angels nor demons, neither the present nor the future, nor any powers, neither height nor depth, nor anything else in all creation, will be able to separate us from the love of God that is in Christ Jesus our Lord (Romans 8:38-39).*

The love that God has for us is difficult to comprehend because it's so different from human love. Human love is often conditional and can end, but God's love is always unconditional and will never end. In fact, God says nothing can separate you from His love. Sin can separate us from God, and it can push you away from Him, but God says nothing will change His love for you. What significance is there to know that nothing can separate you from God's love? Should this affect how you love other people? How?

5. "I have a plan for your life."

"For I know the plans I have for you," declares the LORD, *"plans to prosper you and not to harm you, plans to give you hope and a future. Then you will call upon me and come and pray to me, and I will listen to you. You will seek me and find me when you seek me with all your heart" (Jeremiah 29:11-13).*

Some of us have a master plan for our lives—things we want to accomplish, places we want to go, things we want to do. Others don't have a clue what they want to do or be. But God says he has a plan for you. For you! It's a plan for good and according to this verse from the New Testament, it's a plan that exceeds our greatest goals: *"He who did not spare his own Son, but gave him up for us all—how will he not also, along with him, graciously give us all things" (Romans 8:32)?*

How does knowing that God values you enough to have a plan for your life affect your self worth? In what ways should that verse inspire you and give you confidence?

DISCUSSION GUIDE
Open Up
- Describe the type of person society says is valuable.

- Do you think most teenagers feel valuable? Why or why not?

- It you wanted to help someone feel valuable, what would you do or say? Why?

Dig In
Transition into your study by talking about how most of us don't feel valuable or worthy, so we're tempted to look for worth in people and things that are temporary. Whether it is the affection of a girlfriend, being accepted by a certain group of friends, or being the best at something—all of that fades away. The only place we can find true value and worth is understanding how God sees us.

Read and discuss the five truths God declares about teens.
- What difference do you think it would make in the life of the average teenage guy if he was aware of how God sees him in his life?

- Which of the five do you find the most difficult to believe?

- Which of the five did you connect with the most? Why?

- Do you think God is foolish to love us no matter what? Why?

- Do you have a hard time accepting that God believes in you? Why?

CLOSE OUT
- Which of the five truths do you need to embrace in your own life?

- What difference would it make for you?

- What is one thing you can do this week to help you remember how God values you?

People invest in things they believe are valuable. And because God sent His Son Jesus to die for our sins, He believes we are valuable—He gave us worth.

Romans 5:8 says: *God put his love on the line for us by offering his Son in sacrificial death while we were of no use whatever to him (MSG).*

The struggle for worth and value will be a constant in your life. There will always be some area where you feel vulnerable. Sometimes it will relate to your accomplishments and other times it will relate to your relationships or lack of relationships. Our culture feeds off this weakness.

The only way to combat it time and time again is to remember where your true worth and value comes from. Not from a girl. Not from your strength. Not from your success. Not from your job. Not from what you have. It all comes from the One who gave you worth.

TIP:
It may take an extra "push" to avoid church answers, but it's worth the effort, long-term for your group and for the guys.

Go back through the list on the outline and have each guy share what it means to "hear" God say those things about them. Are there any of those statements that are hard for them to believe? Encourage students to avoid the standard church answers and personalize their response.

Close your session in prayer, asking God to give each one of us a deeper understanding of the worth and value He places on us.

HANGING WITH GOD AT THE MALL

PRIMARY SCRIPTURES

Genesis 2,
Psalm 51:5-6,
Jeremiah 24:7

OBJECTIVES

• Understand the importance of the relationships that surround us.
• Give our relationships the priority they deserve.
• Learn to accept and work on our relationship with God every day.

OVERVIEW

We can't survive without relationships. Some of us enjoy big crowds more than others, but none of us can survive alone. It is part of the way God wired us from the beginning. That is why God and Adam walked through the Garden of Eden together. They actually hung out, just like you and your friends do. They walked and talked and were friends. But God also saw that Adam was lonely, that he needed someone like him to be with.

In Genesis 2:18 God said, *"It is not good for the man to be alone. I will make a helper suitable for him."* And God created Eve from Adam's rib as a companion for him.

In this lesson we want to look at the importance of our relationship with God. Even though Adam had a close relationship with God, he still struggled with making God a priority. After Jesus' sacrifice on the cross, God wants to "walk in the garden" with us. He wants to get to know us, to love us, to be with us. What an incredible gift, and yet it is something we often neglect.

TIP:
Depending on your group, you may have guys "slamming" each other verbally. This lesson could be a powerful experience for your group.

As important as relationships are to teenage guys, they tend to struggle with them. For example, they will make fun of their best friend in front of people or treat girls with disrespect. Today we want to focus on ways to strengthen their relationship with God. This is important and is the catalyst to helping young men improve all of their other relationships. If young men learn to spend time with God and get to know His character and goodness, that will rub off on their other relationships as the same characteristics of a healthy relationship with God apply to all relationships in life.

KEY ELEMENTS OF A HEALTHY RELATIONSHIP

1. Establish and maintain an open line of communication.

How honest are you in your conversations with God?

David was at his lowest point when he committed adultery with Bathsheba and murdered her husband to cover it up. The prophet Nathan was sent by God to call him out on it. In the process of realizing just how far he had gone, David cried out to God. After working hard to cover things up David recognized that it was most important for him to be honest with God.

TIP:
If the guys in your group aren't familiar with this story, pause and read 2 Samuel 11 and 12.

David said, *For I was born a sinner—yes, from the moment my mother conceived me. But you desire honesty from the womb teaching me wisdom even there (Psalm 51:5-6).*

2. Learn new things about one another.

God has an advantage over each one of us here, so developing this area of the relationship falls more on our shoulders than His. But here's the deal—as much as you think you already know about God, you've only scratched the surface.

You think you know God loves you? You'll find time and time again that you consistently underestimate just how far and deep that love is. You think you know God's grace? You'll consistently experience wonder and amazement at just how forgiving God is.

This relationship with God is just that—a relationship. It's not gathering more info; it's learning about Him and yourself.

God says: *"I will give them a heart to know me, that I am the LORD. They will be my people, and I will be their God, for they will return to me with all their heart"* (Jeremiah 24:7). Doesn't that verse sound like we're in a relationship with God?

So how do we get to know God better? We dig into His Word. When we open the Bible we learn three things: who God is, who we are, and how God wants us to act.

We also learn simply by experiencing life as a follower of God, by trusting Him and seeing His promises come true in our own lives.

3. Spend time together.
Who are your best friends? They are likely the people you spend the most time with. If you didn't talk to a friend for a month, they would think you were no longer interested in them. In the same way, you can't expect to have a good relationship with God if you never talk to Him.

God needs to be our #1 relationship, period. That means we need to make sure we spend time with Him as much as we would a good friend.

DISCUSSION GUIDE
Open Up
- What are the three most important relationships in your life?

- If your best friend didn't talk to you for a month what would you think?

- What helps a relationship grow?

TIP:
Prayer is our ongoing conversation with God. Help the guys grasp the simplicity of that thought.

Dig In
Transition into your study by talking about how our relationship with God needs to be the most important one in our life. It's easy to lose track of keeping our relationship with God healthy in the mix of friends, parents and girlfriends. But the more time we spend with God the more those other relationships will benefit. God wants us to know Him, to walk with Him, just like He and Adam walked in the Garden of Eden.

Read and discuss Key Elements of a Healthy Relationship.
- Is there anything else you think is important to a good relationship? Why?

- How important is it to you that your friends, parents, and girlfriend are honest with you?

- Do you think that kind of honesty is easy? Why?

- Why is it good to be honest, even if it means admitting you did something wrong?

- What does it mean to you that God wants to know you personally?

CLOSE OUT
- What is one thing you learned today that you didn't know before?

- Of the three key elements, which one is hardest for you in your relationship with God? Why?

- What is one thing you could do this week to improve in the area you need help on, specifically in your relationship with God?

WHAT WOULD "GOD'S STRONGEST MAN" CONTEST LOOK LIKE?

PRIMARY SCRIPTURES

2 Corinthians 11:30,
2 Corinthians 12:10,
James 1:2-4

OBJECTIVES

- Investigate the source and expression of true strength.
- Understand how we are supposed to build strength.
- Begin strength training.

OVERVIEW

Many guys think the amount of weight you can lift in the gym is the true test of strength. For others, it's how hard they can hit the running back or how long they can run without stopping. It may appear that strength building is limited to the athletic world, but some of the strongest people never set foot in a gym.

They are found in hospitals.

They are found in nursing homes.

They sit in wheelchairs.

They work in a cubicle.

> **TIP:**
> Do all your guys belong to the same gym? Does your church have weights, or do you have equipment at home? This could be a great way of teaching this particular lesson in a non-traditional setting or context.

Strength isn't measured in body mass or barbell weight. Strength is larger than the size of your pecs. Some of the weakest guys fill out their T-shirts, but they crumble when life gets hard. A true man is built through his response to life's difficult and painful experiences, not how many hours he puts in the gym. Resistance builds strength. The more we rely on God and resist giving up, the stronger we get.

HOW DOES A GUY DEVELOP TRUE STRENGTH?

1. A guy gets strong by recognizing the source of strength: God.

God says: *"Was I too weak to save you? Is that why the house is silent and empty when I come home? Is it because I have no power to rescue? No, that is not the reason! For I can speak to the sea and make it dry! I can turn rivers into deserts covered with dying fish"* (Isaiah 50:2).

In other words, God says, "I've got the power."

2. A guy gets strong when he's weak.

This one doesn't make much sense, does it? It's one of those weird Christian opposites. You know what we're talking about? Lose your life to find it. Give up everything to gain a lot.

The apostle Paul was a tough guy. He endured jail (Acts 5:18-25), angry mobs (Acts 22), shipwrecks (Acts 27), and even a snake bite (Acts 28:1-5). But Paul wasn't proud of his own strength. In fact, he knew that if it wasn't for God's strength, he wouldn't have made it through anything. He told the Christians in Corinth: *"If I must boast, I would rather boast about the things that show how weak I am"* (2 Corinthians 11:30).

Since I know it is all for Christ's good, I am quite content with my weaknesses and with insults, hardships, persecutions, and calamities. For when I am weak, then I am strong (2 Corinthians 12:10).

Why is recognizing your weakness important? Because when you do, you realize you need help and you're willing to rely on God's strength.

3. A guys gets strong during tough times.

Wondering why life can get so hard? It could be that God wants to build you up.

James 1:2-4 says: *"Dear brothers and sisters, whenever trouble comes your way, let it be an opportunity for joy. For when your faith is tested, your endurance has a chance to grow. So let it grow, for when your endurance is fully developed, you will be strong in character and ready for anything (NLT)."*

We learn through tough times—we learn what to do and what not to do. But most of all, we learn to trust God with our weakest moments so that His strength can be seen by all.

ADDITIONAL RESOURCES (OPTIONAL)

Show an exercise DVD or video. If you can't find one you want to use at Blockbuster, then ask around—most people have them buried somewhere in their video collections. It would be great to also pull out an Ab Roller or ThighMaster or any other TV-advertised fitness miracle. Then have your guys do the routine for the first 5-10 minutes of your group time. It is okay if they make fun of it. But do the best you can to find the absolutely hardest routine you can find—and then laugh together at the results.

DISCUSSION GUIDE

Open Up

• Who is the strongest person you know? What makes them strong?

• Are there different kinds of strength? If yes, what do you think they are?

• How would you like to be strong?

Dig In

Transition into your study by talking about the differences between bicep strength and the true strength God wants to develop in us—the kind of strength Jesus showed.

Read and discuss the three ways a guy can train for true strength.
• What do you think of God's method of building true strength in us?

• Is there a time in your life that you have had to use true strength?

TIP:
Use a dumbbell or weights to emphasize the role of resistance in physical strength training.

• What is the difference between true strength and the strength most guys look for?

• How important is strength to the average guy?

CLOSE OUT

- What is something new you learned about strength building that you didn't know before?

- What is one thing you can do this week to start building God's strength in your life?

HOW TO KEEP THE GIRL AND NOT LOSE GOD

PRIMARY SCRIPTURES

Genesis 2:19-22,
Matthew 22:37-40,
1 Timothy 5:1-2

OBJECTIVES

- Investigate what a God-honoring relationship with a girl looks like.
- Apply what we find in our current and/or future relationships.

OVERVIEW

Last session, we talked about how a guy develops strength. A guy gets strong when he realizes just how weak he is and how much he needs to rely on God. But life provides plenty of opportunities for a guy to get tripped up, and he can either deal with those situations head on, or he can stumble over them. The challenge is, one of the obstacles looks and smells really nice: girls.

There's something about girls that can shut down a guy's brain. It doesn't mean relating to girls should just be a cerebral activity, but your brain should be just as involved as your heart. Another important item: girls are not the enemy. In fact, God created woman because He knew Adam needed companionship that he wasn't finding in the garden.

Now the LORD God had formed out of the ground all the beasts of the field and all the birds of the air. He brought them to the man to see what he would name them; and whatever the man called each living creature, that was its name. So the man gave names to all the livestock, the birds of the air and all the beasts of the field. But for Adam no suitable helper was found. So the LORD God caused the man to fall into a deep sleep; and while he was sleeping, he took one of the man's ribs and closed up the place with flesh.

Then the LORD God made a woman from the rib he had taken out of the man, and he brought her to the man (Genesis 2:19-22).

Girls weren't designed to hurt us. In fact, God created them to be teammates. And just like guys uniquely reflect God in certain ways, so do girls. We need girls. Girls need us. But most of all, we all need God.

LEADER'S STUDY

HOW DOES A GUY RELATE TO GIRLS IN A WAY THAT DOESN'T TRIP HIM UP?
1. Treat women the way the Bible says we should.
Two verses that provide great instruction:

Jesus said: *"Love the Lord your God with all your passion and prayer and intelligence." This is the most important, the first on any list. But there is a second to set alongside it: "Love others as well as you love yourself. These two commands are pegs; everything in God's Law and the Prophets hangs from them" (Matthew 22:37-40 MSG).*

A lot of people refer to that verse when they're talking about living out their faith, but they also need to apply when it comes to dealing with the opposite sex. Jesus doesn't say to only love God; we should also love other people.

The second verse that gives great advice on how to treat girls is found in 1 Timothy 5:1-2: *"Treat younger men as brothers, older women as mothers, and younger women as sisters, with absolute purity."*

Sister? Are we kidding you? No way. Check out these words from the book *Sex 180*:

"Recognizing and honoring the family bonds that we have in Christ can raise some significant protective walls in relationships. Seeing another person in the context of their bigger story—their individuality, their family, their skills—helps us see the object of our affection less as an object and more as another human being."

2. Remember that girls are not designed to be a substitute for God.

In the movie *Jerry Maguire*, Tom Cruise spouts off a line that has made girls swoon and encouraged guys to add it to their vocabulary. He says to Renee Zellweger, "You complete me." Sounds nice, doesn't it?

This is one of the biggest lies around. Nobody can complete you. No matter how great they are, no matter how much you love them and love being around them, no one person can be everything that you need or want in your life. God didn't create Eve to bring permanent satisfaction to Adam. He created her to be a helper. Remember the verse we just read?

But for Adam no suitable helper was found. So the LORD God caused the man to fall into a deep sleep; and while he was sleeping, he took one of the man's ribs and closed up the place with flesh. Then the LORD God made a woman from the rib he had taken out of the man, and he brought her to the man (Genesis 2:20-22).

3. Step up and be a leader in your relationship.

Our culture talks a lot about girl power and there are many positives about it. But one bad thing is that it encourages guys to be passive.

This does not mean that guys should order women around like employees and dominate the relationship to make sure it's all about them. No way. There's nothing biblical about that. The Bible says that we should love others and that guys should follow Jesus' servant lead and love their wives like He loves the church (Ephesians 5:22-33).

ADDITIONAL RESOURCES (OPTIONAL)

To introduce today's lesson, read the following list of cheesy pick-up lines men use to get a woman's attention:

TIP:
Have a lot of fun with this! Use laughter to teach a powerful lesson on how weird we guys can be around women!

- Can I borrow a quarter? ["What for?"] I want to call my mom and tell her I just met the girl of my dreams. OR: I want to call your mother and thank her.
- Congratulations! You've been voted "Most Beautiful Girl in This Room" and the grand prize is me!
- Hi, I just wanted to give you the satisfaction of turning me down; go ahead say no.

- I have had a really bad day and it always makes me feel better to see a pretty girl smile. So, would you smile for me?
- I hope you know CPR, because you take my breath away!
- I just wanted to show this rose how incredibly beautiful you are!!
- I know milk does a body good, but baby, how much have you been drinking?
- Oh my sweet darling! For a moment I thought I had died and gone to heaven. Now I see that I am very much alive, and heaven has been brought to me.
- Overheard in our computer lab: Just because computers are incompatible, doesn't mean we are.
- You're ugly but you intrigue me.

Ask the guys in your group to come up with some of their own cheesy pick-up lines.

DISCUSSION GUIDE
Open Up
- Tell a story from your school of how a guy/girl relationship has gone bad.

- What do you think messed things up for them?

- What would most teenagers say a guy's role is in a romantic relationship?

Dig In
Transition into your study by talking about how as much as we desire a good relationship with a girl, it can also be difficult. A lot of times we get our priorities mixed up and God ends up taking a back seat when we end up in one with our girlfriend. We need to figure out how God wants us to treat girls while honoring Him at the same time.

Read and discuss the three ways God says we are to be God-honoring in how we treat girls:
- What are some ways we can show love to others as the Bible instructs?

TIP:
Respect is crucial for healthy relationships, especially relationships with girls!

- How can we apply some of those principles to how we relate to girls?

- If you have a sister, how would you want a guy to treat her?

- What are some ways guy needs to "take the lead" in a relationship? What does "take the lead" not mean in a relationship?

- What do you have to sacrifice to have a healthy God-honoring relationship with a girl?

CLOSE OUT

- What is something new you have learned from this lesson?

- Is it worth it to try and have a relationship with a girl the way that God says? Why or Why not?

- What is one thing that needs to change in your priorities and/or expectations to help you have a God-honoring relationship with a girl?

START WINNING THE BATTLE AGAINST LUST

PRIMARY SCRIPTURES

Ephesians 4:19; 5:3,
Matthew 5:29,
Psalm 139:3

OBJECTIVES

- Identify the results of pursuing lustful thoughts.
- Explore what the Bible says about how to defeat lust.
- Support one another in our fight against lust.

OVERVIEW

Have you ever come home from school or practice and been so incredibly hungry? Instead of just grabbing an apple or a granola bar, you start shoving whatever is in the fridge into your mouth. You go from one plastic container to the next, devouring every leftover without mold until there's nothing left to eat. While your family may be happy that there's no more leftovers in the fridge, your stomach is asking, "Why did you do that?" You ate stuff that you never thought you would eat to satisfy your hunger.

Lust is like that. It's never satisfied; it always wants more. Whether it's a physical, spiritual, or emotional need, lust can drive any guy to do things he never thought he would.

TIP:

This is a "biggie" topic for any guys groups. Remember that some guys will talk openly, while others will just laugh or shut down.

Paul wrote about people caught in lust's trap in his letter to the church in Ephesus: *"Having lost all sensitivity, they have given themselves over to sensuality as to indulge in every kind of impurity, with a continual lust for more (Ephesians 4:19)."*

Joshua Harris, in his book *Not Even a Hint* (Multnomah Books) wrote about the greed of lust:

"You won't be able to fantasize enough to quench lust. You won't be able to sleep with enough people. You won't be able to view enough pornography. You can gorge yourself on lust, but you're always going to be hungry . . . "

LEADER'S STUDY

Ask a group of guys what their biggest struggle is, and the one answer you'll hear the most is lust. A guy's battle with lust shows up in different ways, but for all of them, it is a struggle.

So how do you live in such a way that you don't constantly feel like you're being controlled by your lust? Here are some clues from the Bible.

1. Don't give it a chance.

Paul wrote to the church in Ephesus: *"Among you there must not be even a hint of sexual immorality, or of any kind of impurity, or of greed, because these are improper for God's holy people"* (Ephesians 5:3). In other words, when lust starts knocking on your door, don't open it.

TIP:
Link this back to the lesson on strength and weights—the role of resistance.

If you notice a hot girl running alongside the road in a top that's barely there, don't look. If you've already seen her, don't take a second glance. It's the second look that will get you. If you're flipping channels and run across a movie that you know has an explicit sex scene, don't sit there and justify watching the movie because you want to know the story. Make the choice to be victorious over lust and change the channel or turn off the TV—that is a sign of strength.

2. Go to extreme measures.

Jesus says: *"Let's not pretend this is easier than it really is. If you want to live a morally pure life, here's what you have to do: You have to blind your right eye the moment you catch it in a lustful leer. You have to choose to live one-eyed or else be dumped on a moral trash pile"* (Matthew 5:29 MSG).

Is that what Jesus expects, self-mutilation? No. But He's using an extreme example to make an extreme point—that lust will consume your life.

What parts of your life are feeding your lust? No matter how much you want to believe you can handle it, deep down you know there are things in your life that need to be cut out. It's not your eyes, but it could be your MySpace account, or your music, or the movies you rent. Whatever it is, Jesus said go to extreme measures to cut those things out of your life. Break up. Unplug. Delete the account. But do what you need to do to cut whatever it is out of your life.

3. Get to the heart of what's really going on.

At the heart of a lust struggle is huge trust issue—we don't believe that God's going to deliver all He promises. We're not sure if sex inside marriage is going to be as great as people say it is. We're not really that sure we'll survive if we don't watch certain movies or visit particular websites. We're not so sure we can really trust God.

Ask God to reveal what's really going on inside you. Psalm 139:23 says: *"Search me, O God, and know my heart."* Ask Him to show you what need you're trying to get met on your own. What are you not trusting Him to take care of? What truth of His are you just not sure you're buying into?

ADDITIONAL RESOURCES (OPTIONAL)

TIP:
The scenes of Gollum being transformed early in *The Return of the King* are especially powerful.

One of the best visuals for this topic is any of the three *Lord of the Rings* films: *The Fellowship of the Ring, The Two Towers,* or *The Return of the King*. The lust for the ring in all of these films, particularly with the character of Gollum, shows just how far a desire for something can go.

Another great clip to show is the interaction between Edmund and the Witch in *The Chronicles of Narnia: The Lion, the Witch, and the Wardrobe*. Edmund's desire for more Turkish delight leads him to forget everything good he knows just to feed his desire for more.

DISCUSSION GUIDE
Open Up
• What's a good definition for lust?

• In what ways does lust reveal itself in a guy's life?

• Why do you think lust is such a struggle for guys?

Dig In
Transition into your study by talking about how every guy deals with lust. It may not always be at the same level, or because of the same experiences, but every guy needs to know it is a weakness that needs to be monitored. God doesn't want us to lose this fight with lust. In fact, the salvation that Jesus brought through His death was supposed to free us from sin and its power.

Read and discuss the Clues the Bible gives us in defeating lust:
• Which is more important to most guys: having a God-honoring relationship with a girl or just having a relationship the way everyone else does? Explain.

• What would most guys have to give up in order to defeat lust? Is it possible? How?

• What effect do you think lust has on a relationship? On your future marriage?

• If you had a daughter that was a teenager how would you want her dates to treat her? Is that any different from how you now are treating someone else's daughter?

• How does our exposure to TV, movies, music and other media channels set us up to fail when it comes to lust?

CLOSE OUT
• Which of the three "Clues" resonates with you the most? Why?

• What are some ways that you can start fighting lust this week?

• What are some ways as a group we can encourage each other to fight lust every week?

LEARNING TO WALK THE PATH OF A MAN

PRIMARY SCRIPTURES

Matthew 18:3,
1 Corinthians 13:11,
Luke 22:60-62,
John 21,
Psalm 34:18

OBJECTIVES

- Recognize that walking the path of a man is challenging and will be costly.
- Look at how the Bible says we should respond to those challenges.
- Identify our wounds and practical ways to respond to them.

OVERVIEW

Cutting words. Abuse. Failure. Frustration. Tragedy. Walking the path of a man is laden with events that hurt us. It would be nice if there was a method, or more likely a miracle, that we could use to avoid pain and struggle from our lives, but there isn't. The only power we have is choice. The choice to respond in a positive way or the choice to hold on to your hurt and let it have power over you.

Some people let hurtful events affect them for their entire lives. They never are able to move forward because they allow their past to rule them. God doesn't want that for us. God doesn't bring pain into our lives, but He wants to be a source of healing that brings good out of the bad. God uses the pain in our lives to help us become stronger and more faithful while learning to trust Him more. That is the path of becoming the man God wants you to be.

LEADER'S STUDY

If you're carrying around baggage from the past, it's hard to move forward. Sometimes it's a matter of simply getting over it. Other times it's a matter of allowing God to heal deep wounds.

Whatever the circumstance, for a guy to be all God made him to be, he needs to make four choices.

1. Choose to leave your little boy ways behind.

While Jesus said that we need to have faith like a child (Matthew 18:3), He isn't saying that we should keep acting like one. In fact, the apostle Paul said: *"When I was a child, I talked like a child, I thought like a child, I reasoned like a child. When I became a man, I put childish ways behind me" (1 Corinthians 13:11).*

What are some ways that a little boy acts versus how a man acts? For example, a little boy may expect others to take care of him and feed him. A man figures out how to feed himself. If you want to put your boyish ways behind, then you need to start feeding yourself spiritually. You need to quit relying solely on a sermon, a song, or even your friends to feed you spiritually. You need to get one on one with God and let Him feed you directly through His Word. Yes, you need to read your Bible.

TIP:
Our goal is to see teens own their faith.

2. Choose to realize that your failures shape you just as much as your successes.

The apostle Peter walked with Jesus. He saw Jesus work miracles. He heard Jesus teach. He not only heard about Jesus' great love and compassion, he experienced it. Yet when it came time for Peter to step up and stand up for Jesus, he bailed—and he failed, big time. In fact, he said three different times that he didn't know Jesus.

Peter replied, "Man, I don't know what you're talking about!" Just as he was speaking, the rooster crowed. The Lord turned and looked straight at Peter. Then Peter remembered the word the Lord had spoken to him: "Before the rooster crows today, you will disown me three times." And he went outside and wept bitterly (Luke 22:60-62).

When Peter failed, he went into a deep depression. In fact, instead of picking up Jesus' mission, he went back to his job as a fisherman. But a resurrected Jesus met Peter where he was. He reminded Peter of who He was and what He was about. He restored Peter through His words and He also empowered him to move forward. (Read John 21.)

3. Choose to heal from your wounds and move forward.

Life hurts. There are things that each of us has done that we regret. But sometimes others have done things that really wound us and keep us stuck in the past. It could be a dad who just wasn't there in the way that you needed him to be. It could be a girl who just chewed up your heart and spit it out. It could be a friend who you thought you could trust, but completely proved otherwise. Whatever the case, there's one key promise from God: *"The LORD is close to the brokenhearted and saves those who are crushed in spirit" (Psalm 34:18).*

God's not scared of wounds, and He has the power to heal you. Psalm 147:3 says: *"He heals the brokenhearted and binds up their wounds."*

4. Choose to quit believing lies to move forward.
Words haunt us. Whether they were said carelessly, in anger, or even in your own head, there are words inside each of us that cripple us.

Stupid. Idiot. Failure. Ugly. Worthless. Reject. Second-rate. Someone in your life may have actually said those things to you. Or you may have been around people who certainly made you feel that way.

But guess what? Those aren't the words God says about you. Those are straight from another source—Satan. And he's never been known as a reliable source.

Jesus says: *"He was a murderer from the beginning, not holding to the truth, for there is no truth in him. When he lies, he speaks his native language, for he is a liar and the father of lies" (John 8:44).*

DISCUSSION GUIDE
Open Up
- What's the worst/funniest story you have heard of how a girl dumped a guy?

- What are some other things teenage guys have to deal with?

- How do you think the average teenager guy responds when he's been hurt emotionally or socially?

Dig In
Transition into your study by talking about how pain and hardship in life are unavoidable. We all have events and people in our lives who have hurt us. God doesn't do these things to us; instead He wants to use them to make us better people.

Read and discuss the four choices:

- What is a little boy way to react to a girl dumping you? What is the way God would have you respond? Which is harder?

- What are some other little boy reactions to hurtful events?

- What is the "right way" to respond to failure?

- Do you trust God with your hurts? Why or why not?

- What is one wound you have from your past, and how have you responded to it so far?

CLOSE OUT

- What are the roadblocks for most teenage guys that keep them from responding the way they should to hurtful events?

- Identify one hurt you are still holding onto. Come up with two action steps you can take this week.

DON'T PASS THE BUCK, STEP UP!

PRIMARY SCRIPTURES

Matthew 25: 35-40,
Hebrews 13:3,
Isaiah 1:17,
Matthew 5:14

OBJECTIVES

- Explore our responsibility in larger needs and tragedies.
- Work together to step up to the Bible's expectations.

OVERVIEW

When we hear about different tragedies in the world, like the child sex trade in Asia or AIDS pandemic and the orphans it has produced, our stomachs can begin to feel queasy, and we wonder, "Why doesn't anyone do anything?" The problem is so evil and tragic that it is hard for us to feel like we could make a difference. We get overwhelmed, which paralyzes us, and eventually we just forget. It never occurs to us that we might be the ones who need to take care of the situation.

Jesus said that the two greatest commands in the entire Bible—the two that all the others hang on—are loving God and loving other people. Even if we don't know how, even if it seems too big, when we see a need, hurt or tragedy that is pulling at our heart we need to trust God and see what we can do. Whether it is in Indonesia, or next door, we need to take action and start caring.

TIP:
Social action is a hot topic for this generation. It's a great way to talk about putting faith into action.

LEADER'S STUDY

Why should you care? Because serving others is one of the biggest ways to get your heart lined up with Jesus. It's where His was. Check out this verse: *"A vast crowd was there as he stepped from the* boat, and he had compassion on them because they were like sheep without a shepherd" (Mark 6:34 NLT).

So how do you start doing that? How do you live in such a way that shows that you care about what's going on around you?

1. When you see a need, take action.

Jesus said: "'For I was hungry and you gave me something to eat, I was thirsty and you gave me something to drink, I was a stranger and you invited me in, I needed clothes and you clothed me, I was sick and you looked after me, I was in prison and you came to visit me.'

Then the righteous will answer him, 'Lord, when did we see you hungry and feed you, or thirsty and give you something to drink? When did we see you a stranger and invite you in, or needing clothes and clothe you? When did we see you sick or in prison and go to visit you?'

The King will reply, 'I tell you the truth, whatever you did for one of the least of these brothers of mine, you did for me'" (Matthew 25:35-40).

These verses aren't just about taking care of the homeless. They're about noticing people around you, getting your eyes on someone other than yourself. But not only do you see what people need, just as Jesus did, you are moved to do something about it. Whether it's through helping someone directly or connecting them with someone who can, Jesus says when you see a need, take care of it.

2. When you hear about something horrible in the news, respond together.

Paul wrote: "Remember those in prison as if you were their fellow prisoners, and those who are mistreated as if you yourselves were suffering" (Hebrews 13:3).

Don't just let the latest headlines roll in and out of your brain; put yourself in that situation. What would it be like if that happened to you? How would you want someone to respond?

If your family's home was burned down, what would you want people to do for you? How would you feel if someone went the extra mile and gave you the best they could—a new shirt, a CD player—something an emergency shelter couldn't give?

If it's a big international headline, think about how you could respond. If it's war in another country, find out how you can sponsor a child in that country through World Vision (www.worldvision.org) or Compassion International (www.compassion.com). If it's a story about child slavery or prostitution, raise money for the International Justice Mission (www.ijm.org), an organization that fights for the rights of people around the world.

Take another look at the newspapers and magazines from the beginning of this session. Tear out a page and distribute them to the guys in your group, asking them to pray specifically about that situation and to ask God how they can respond to that need.

The Bible says: *"Learn to do good. Seek justice. Help the oppressed. Defend the orphan. Fight for the rights of widows" (Isaiah 1:17 NLT).*

3. Be known for being a Christian.

Jesus said: *"You are the light of the world. A city on hill cannot be hidden"* (Matthew 5:14).

Want to know what moves people genuinely? Not a great debate on how "right" you are about a particular issue. What moves people is seeing someone genuinely care about others. It's what we love about Jesus.

ADDITIONAL RESOURCES (OPTIONAL)

Bring in some newspapers and news magazines (*Time, Newsweek,* etc.). Hand one out to each student and ask every guy to find the top three articles that most capture their attention. Have each guy share what he found and why that particular article captured his attention.

Now, as a group, go back through and note the articles that tie in with things going on in the world and in your community that show people in need or hurting. How many of those articles were missed or found by the guys in your group?

DISCUSSION GUIDE
Open Up
- What are the biggest world problems you can think of?

- Why is it hard for us to figure out how to help solve those problems?

- Who do you think are the ones who are supposed to help with those big needs?

Dig In
Transition into your study by talking about how God wants to use us to address the big, little and in-between needs of the world. But that most of us, when it comes down to it, have a really hard time caring enough to take action. Our video game systems, movies on the weekends, and TiVo at home keep us happy and we eventually forget about the needs that we have seen around us.

Read and discuss the three ways we start caring about the world:
- Who do you know or heard about that has taken action toward a specific need, whether local or global? What was the result?

- When you help someone, are they the only ones who get something from it?

- What does God do in you when you are willing to serve?

- Why can it be hard to be known as a "Christian"?

- What does it mean in your life to live and love in a way that it is obvious to everyone that you follow Jesus? How does that idea make you feel?

CLOSE OUT
- What things might you need to sacrifice in order to be used by God in a way that helps those around you?

TIP:
This can help launch an outreach effort for your whole youth group.

- For the next week, figure out one thing your group can do to serve a need in your community.

TAKE THE LEAD

PRIMARY SCRIPTURES

Exodus 3:11-12, 4:1, 4:10-15

OBJECTIVES

- Learn leadership lessons by looking at Moses' life.
- Understand the role of a leader.
- Take steps to become the leader God is looking for.

OVERVIEW

There may be someone who enjoys the spotlight more, has better organizational skills, or a more persuasive personality than you, but everyone has moments when they are called to lead. Every guy—with every personality type—will have an opportunity to lead.

The opportunities to lead aren't always big things. Maybe you're asked to lead a club at school, lead a Bible study at youth group, or lead your band. In his book, *Summoned to Lead* (Zondervan), author Leonard Sweet said: "We're all 'players' in life. Yet sometimes life summons 'players' to be 'leaders.' It may happen only once or twice in life. Sometimes life takes shape in such a way that a player is like the missing piece of a puzzle; the exact fit for the situation. Up to that point, the jagged pieces of your life don't seem to fit into any significant pattern. But then life calls you and summons you forth. A player in life becomes a leader, and even 'born leaders' find themselves following the summoned leader."

When those moments come along, you may be tempted to sit back and wait for someone else to provide leadership, possibly someone with more skills or experience than you or someone others may identify more as a "leader." But don't wait. Sometimes you just have to do something. Sometimes, whether you think you have what it takes or not, God thinks you're the man for the job.

LEADER'S STUDY

It's not every day that you're going about your regular routine when you spy a bush that's burning flames but not being destroyed. But that describes Moses' experience one day while he was shepherding sheep.

TIP:
The four excuses below are remarkably still with us today.

God summoned Moses to lead—in a big way. But Moses didn't think of himself as a "leader." He believed the only thing he should be leading were sheep. And he had a lot of reasons why God should choose someone else. Let's listen in on the conversation.

1. "Who am I to appear before Pharaoh?"

Moses asked God, *"How can you expect me to lead the Israelites out of Egypt?"* *(Exodus 3:11 NLT).*

Moses wasn't exactly the best candidate to talk with Pharaoh as he killed a man the last time he was in Egypt. He was a fugitive from justice and therefore carried a lot of baggage.

But as awful as Moses thought he was, none of his past surprised God when He summoned Moses to lead. But not only that, He told Moses: *"I will be with you. And this will serve as proof that I have sent you: When you have brought the Israelites out of Egypt, you will return here to worship God at this very mountain"* *(Exodus 3:12 NLT).*

Some guys think they can't be used by God because they made some bad, sinful choices in their past. But God never uses perfect people; He uses people who realize they most need God.

2. Who is going to follow me?

"Look, they won't believe me! They won't do what I tell them. They'll just say, 'The LORD never appeared to you'" *(Exodus 4:1 NLT).*

If you step out and do something God is calling you to do, people may think you're crazy, or the more politely phrased "extreme." Remember, we live in a culture that doesn't really go for extreme—unless we're watching it on TV for entertainment. It's okay to care about something, just don't care about it a lot. But if God calls you to do something, people are going to think you've gone too far.

But our relationship with Jesus isn't about making a comfortable life for ourselves. It's not about building our own kingdoms; it's about following the true King. It's about living in such a way that shows who truly rules and reigns in our lives.

3. I don't have what it takes!
"O Lord, I'm just not a good speaker. I never have been, and I'm not now, even after you have spoken to me. I'm clumsy with words" (Exodus 4:10 NLT).

So many times when we're faced with something new and scary, we're quick to take inventory of all the ways we don't measure up for the task. But not everything God asks you to do will be something that you're an expert at. There are times when your skills and abilities may or may not fit perfectly with the task, but God is more concerned about your obedience to His call than your level of comfort.

But remember, God's strength shows up in our weakness. Whatever we lack, whatever our limits are, His abilities go so much further.

In response to Moses' excuse, God said: *"Who makes people so they can speak or not speak, hear or not hear, see or not see? Is it not I, the LORD? Now go, and do as I have told you. I will help you speak well, and I will tell you what to say" (Exodus 4:11-12 NLT).*

4. I don't want to!
"Moses again pleaded, "Lord, please! Send someone else" (Exodus 4:12 NLT).

You're not always going to be pumped about leading. There will be times when you wish someone else would do it. You'll be looking around, pleading, "Someone, anyone?"

The reality is that God doesn't need our help to do anything. But He invites us to be part of what He's doing in the world. God let Moses off the hook and sent along a helper. And while He allowed Moses to face Pharaoh with a sidekick,

God still told Moses that He would be the point man for His communication with the Israelites.

"I will help both of you to speak clearly, and I will tell you what to do. Aaron will be your spokesman to the people, and you will be as God to him, telling him what to say" (Exodus 4:15-16 NLT).

ADDITIONAL RESOURCES (OPTIONAL)
Show the following clip from the movie *The Prince of Egypt* (Dreamworks):

Using a burning bush to get Moses' attention, God asks Moses to lead the Israelites to freedom in the Promised Land. At first Moses can't believe the Lord is talking to him, but once God makes His identity known, Moses struggles to believe that God wants him to free the Israelites. Isn't somebody else better equipped for this job?

Start: 0:42:47 Moses notices a sheep wandering off and follows it.
Stop: 0:47:47 Moses stands beside the unharmed bush in awe.
(Source: Videos that Teach 2 by Doug Fields & Eddie James, Zondervan)

DISCUSSION GUIDE
Open Up
• Name some leaders that you respect.

• What makes them good leaders?

• Do you see yourself as a leader? Why or why not?

TIP:
Talk about some of your "unexpected" opportunities to lead, especially if you had some as a teenager.

Dig In
Transition into your study by saying that even though some of us aren't natural born leaders, it doesn't change the fact that God will ask us to lead as men. Not all of us will be the President, but plenty of us will have families, relationships and even a Bible study to lead. For some of us that is a little scary, and we have questions as to whether we are the right guy. Moses asked the same thing.

Read and discuss Moses' encounter with the burning bush:

- Moses had a hard time believing that God could work through him. Why do so many of struggle with believing that?

- What are some things from your past that make you afraid to step up and lead?

- How much do you allow the opinions of others to affect what you do or don't do?

- Has there been a time when you had the opportunity to lead but didn't? Share about that time and what you wish you would have done differently.

- If God called you to lead in a great way, would you trust him to show up? Why or why not?

CLOSE OUT

- What are two places in your life that you feel God wants you to show more leadership?

- What is one thing you could do this week to begin showing leadership in one of those areas?

- What are some things you can do that will help you grow as a leader? Which of those will you begin?

FINAL WORD: GET THE RIGHT TOOLS

PRIMARY SCRIPTURES

2 Corinthians
1:21-22,
John 14:26,
Galatians 5:16,
Hebrews 4:12,
Matthew 4:4,
Psalm 37:30; 119:
9-11, 105,
Proverbs 17:17

OBJECTIVES

- Become aware of the tools God has given us to become men.
- Take the necessary steps to make sure we surround ourselves with these tools.

OVERVIEW

Guys love tools. We love to fix problems and have the right tool at the right time to help us out. Let's apply that to our ten-week pursuit at becoming the man God is calling us to be. There are times when we are going to have a problem, and we need to surround ourselves with the right tools for the job.

No one can do life alone—that is setting yourself up for failure. Instead, prepare yourself to succeed. Fill your toolbox with these tools from God: the Holy Spirit, the Bible, Christian brothers, and adult mentors. God never intended us to go through life by ourselves and these tools give us a fighting chance.

LEADER'S STUDY

Here are the four tools God has given us to become men:

TIP:
Consider building something together, if you're that kind of group.

1. The Holy Spirit

When you became a Christian, God placed the Holy Spirit in your life. He lives inside you. The apostle Paul described the Holy Spirit in this way: *"Now it is God who makes both us and you stand firm in Christ. He anointed us, set his seal of ownership on* us, and put his Spirit in our hearts as a deposit, guaranteeing what is to come" (2 Corinthians 1:21-22). In other words, God considered our lives so valuable that He not only paid the price for our sins through Jesus' death, He continued to invest in us by placing the Holy Spirit in our lives.

So what does the Holy Spirit do?

He reminds us of the things we know are true. Jesus said: "The Counselor, the Holy Spirit, whom the Father will send in my name, will teach you all things and will remind you of everything I have said to you" (John 14:26). The Holy Spirit helps us follow Jesus' leadership every moment of every day. We have the choice to obey His voice or follow our own.

2. The Word of God—the Bible
If you've been in the church for a while, you know it's important to read the Bible, but few of us do it consistently.

But let's look at the Bible a little differently. The Bible tells us four things—who God is, who we are, how God relates to us, and how we should relate to God. You'll never be the man you're supposed to be until you start diving into the Bible. It's not just another self-help book to help you live better—it's life itself. It breathes into our dead souls. It's one of the ways God speaks directly to us.

It gives us direction.
"Your word is a lamp to my feet and a light for my path" (Psalm 119:105).

It cuts through the junk of our lives and our world.
"Sharper than any double-edged sword, it penetrates even to dividing soul and spirit, joints and marrow; it judges the thoughts and attitudes of the heart" (Hebrews 4:12).

It provides strength and nourishment.
"Man does not live on bread alone, but on every word that comes from the mouth of God" (Matthew 4:4).

It helps us be the men we are meant to be.
"How can a young man keep his way pure? By living according to your word. I seek you with all my heart; do not let me stray from your commands. I have hidden your word in my heart that I might not sin against you" (Psalm 119:9-11).

3. Christian brothers

A guy needs other guys.

Guys who will be there when needed.

Guys who will be honest.

And guys who will always point one another towards Jesus.

Proverbs 17:17 says: *"A friend is always loyal, and a brother is born to help in time of need."*

4. Adult mentors

We need to learn from a variety of men as there's no perfect person to learn from—including your dad. Every guy has different strengths and weaknesses: One guy can build a house out of a single piece of wood and bucket of nails, another can take $5 and turn it into $1,000.

The Bible encourages us to seek out wise counsel from guys who love Jesus and are living out their faith. Psalm 37:30 says: *"The godly offer good counsel; they know what is right from wrong."*

ADDITIONAL RESOURCES (OPTIONAL)

This is your last session and it's all about making sure a guy has everything he needs in his "toolbox" to be the man God has made him to be.

To start out, bring in some tools that have either unusual uses or are no longer in use. (You may want to ask some of the men in your church who are engineers or mechanics if they have some tools you can borrow.)

Ask your guys to try to guess the real use and purpose of each tool

TIP:
This could be a great way to get men involved as mentors for the guys in your group.

End of Series Idea

As an end to these sessions, give each guy a toolbox. On the inside of the toolbox include note cards with key scripture verses on them. (You may want to use verses from the last 10 sessions.)

You may also want to solicit advice from other men in the church as to what it means to be a man of God and include their comments in the box as well.

In closing, say: "Guys look different. We all have different passions. Different skills. Different interests. Different strengths. But the core of guys is the same. We have a common bond, no matter how different we are from one another, and that's the commitment to lead, whether it's in the school musical, on a sports team, or at home. Be the man God made you to be. Pursue God daily. Invest in your relationship with Him. Read His Word. Serve others. Love other people. Lead."

Read Psalm 139:1-18 in closing.

"O LORD, you have examined my heart and know everything about me. You know when I sit down or stand up. You know my every thought when far away. You chart the path ahead of me and tell me where to stop and rest. Every moment you know where I am. You know what I am going to say even before I say it, LORD. You both precede and follow me. You place your hand of blessing on my head. Such knowledge is too wonderful for me, too great for me to know! I can never escape from your spirit! I can never get away from your presence! If I go up to heaven, you are there; if I go down to the place of the dead, you are there. If I ride the wings of the morning, if I dwell by the farthest oceans, even there your hand will guide me, and your strength will support me. I could ask the darkness to hide me and the light around me to become night—but even in darkness I cannot hide from you. To you the night shines as bright as day. Darkness and light are both alike to you. You made all the delicate, inner parts of my body and knit me together in my mother's womb. Thank you for making me so wonderfully complex! Your workmanship is marvelous—and how well I know it. You watched me as I was being formed in utter seclusion, as I was woven together in the dark of the womb. You saw me before I was born. Every day of my life was recorded in your book. Every moment was laid out before a single day had passed. How precious are your thoughts about me, O God! They are innumerable! I can't even count them; they outnumber the grains of sand! And when I wake up in the morning, you are still with me!" (NLT)

DISCUSSION GUIDE
Open Up
- Tell about a time some guy failed in a big way.

- Why do you think he failed? What lead to his failure?

- What do you think he could have done to avoid that kind of failure?

Dig In
Transition into your study by talking about how guys often set themselves up for failure. They try to be lone rangers, thinking they don't need others, but find out life is impossible on their own. To be the men God called us to be, we need to make sure we have the right tools to help us succeed.

Read and discuss the four tools that help a man succeed:
- Do any of these surprise you? Why?

- If we already know we need to read the Bible, why is it so difficult to do so?

- Is it hard to find guys to trust as brothers?

- If you could have any one person as a mentor, who would you choose? Why?

CLOSE OUT
- Which of the four tools do you use the most? Tell about a time you used that tool.

- Which of the four tools do you find the most difficult to use? Why?

- What is one thing you can do to begin getting more comfortable with that tool?

- What are some ways to find a mentor?

- How have the last ten weeks changed your perception of what it means to be a man?

- What is your one "take away," the one thing that has had a profound effect on you during this series?

> **TIP:**
> Depending on your situation, talk about where you go next. How can the guys help one another grow, even if they're not all in the same small group?

✕ GIRL TALK ✕

BEWARE! ARE YOU SENDING THE RIGHT MESSAGE?

PRIMARY SCRIPTURES

Proverbs 6:25, 11:22, 31:30

OBJECTIVES

- Examine our motives for seeking the perfect appearance.
- Explore the lies that convince us that our appearance is all that we are.
- Discuss the outcome of our decisions about our appearance.

OVERVIEW

Preppy, jock, tomboy, slut, nerd, punk…the list could go on and on identifying the different labels or groups that exist in the world of a teenager. The labels change over time, but the process of labeling doesn't. I can't remember the first time I put someone in a certain "group" based on what they were wearing or how they had their hair done because it feels like I've been doing it my entire life. And I am sure I would be surprised to find out some of the many "groups" I was put into based on other's judgment of my appearance. Why do we think we can really know a person solely based on outward appearance? Can we really be known by our own appearance?

TIP:
Think back to your high school days, however recent or distant. Think about your "label" and the different groups at your school. Most of us have been where your girls are today!

Because celebrities get so much attention, we allow the way they dress and act to influence us. We try to emulate them with hopes of receiving the same type of attention. We want attention and we want to be desirable. What we often forget is we are desirable. God desires us. He loves us no matter what clothes we wear, what kind of make-up we wear or what friends we hang out with. No matter what.

Society says the way we look on the outside determines our character and who we are. God knows our character based on the state of our heart. What we don't always realize is the way we dress and act can reflect the state of our heart.

Charm is deceptive, and beauty is fleeting; but a woman who fears the LORD is to be praised (Proverbs 31:30).

LEADER'S STUDY

Proverbs 6:25, 11:22, 31:30

Let's take a quick look at the scriptures used today in our Bible study:

Proverbs 6:25 – The "her" in this passage is an immoral woman. The writer is telling us not to be blinded by her appearance. Though her outside is captivating and beautiful, something is deeply wrong on the inside.

Proverbs 11:22 – Being too consumed by or "showing off" your appearance is like dressing up a pig in jewelry. You can't disguise what's in your heart—it will find its way out sooner or later.

TIP:

Get some comments from the guys in your church about the traits they look for in girls, and what kind of girls they respect the most.

Proverbs 31:30 – This passage is actually directed at men as the writer is telling a young man how to pick a wife. Don't look for outward beauty because eventually it will fade; instead search for someone whose heart is totally devoted to God.

3 QUESTIONS TO ASK ABOUT YOUR APPEARANCE...

1. Am I trying to hide something?

Am I focusing so much time and energy on what I look like so people will never really notice me? A lot of times we use the exterior to distract people from really knowing us because we are afraid that we aren't good enough. Beware: the message you are sending is that you are only skin deep.

2. What kind of attention am I trying to attract?

Am I making attempts to get people to notice me by wearing things or doing things to myself that I don't necessarily care for? Sometimes when we don't feel so good about ourselves, we think people feel the same way about us, and so we begin to take drastic measures to get the attention we think we so badly need. We are sure that this attention will validate our self-worth and provide us with the love we need. Beware: the message you are sending is that you'll do anything for attention.

3. Do I spend the same amount of time and energy on my heart as I do my appearance?

Am I focusing so much on my outside appearance that I am neglecting the care of my heart and my faith? It's so easy to get sidetracked by "looking good" that before long it becomes all that we think about. We want to be in control and since our appearance is something we can control, we spend all our time and energy on it. However, in the end beauty doesn't last, but our heart does. So it is imperative that we give care and attention to our heart and soul. Beware: the message you are sending is that looking good is worth risking your heart.

ADDITIONAL RESOURCES (OPTIONAL)

The List (Bring a Barbie doll) – Together as a group make a list of the messages that the world has described as perfect. Most of our lives we have been trying to live up to the standard set by a Barbie doll. Did you know that if a real person had the actual measurements of a Barbie she would be so top heavy that she wouldn't be able to stand?

Making the comparisons – Have the students compare the difference of Britney Spears (or any other young "beautiful" celebrity) to Mother Teresa. After completing the list, have the students talk about the realities of what the world ranks as important.

TIP:
Younger girls may not know much about Mother Teresa's life. Do a little research online so you can tell them more about all of the things she did.

DISCUSSION GUIDE
Open Up

- How are people in your school or community "classified"? By their appearance or by their actions?

- What do the media tell us about our appearance?

- How often do you classify people?

- Do you think people send a message with the way they dress or take care of their appearance? Do you believe that boys and girls think the same about appearances?

- What message do you want to be sending with your appearance? Do you think you are sending that message?

Dig In

Transition into your study by explaining the common messages we send with our appearance (that we are only skin deep, that we'll do anything with our appearance for acceptance, and that what is on the outside is more important than the heart). Does everyone in the group agree? If not, why? The Bible teaches that appearances can be deceiving: What's on the outside of a person may not be what's inside their heart. While the world focuses on appearance, God's Word makes it clear that beauty won't last forever but character does. Today we'll explore what God says about focusing on our appearance.

Read and discuss Proverbs 6:25, 11:22, 31:30

- What do you think the word "captivating" means?

- Have you ever been captivated by a person's appearance? In what way? Did you get to know that person? Were their looks deceiving? How?

- Why do you think our society is "blinded" by appearance? What message does that send to you about your appearance?

- Describe how you would react to seeing a pig with an expensive nose ring. How does that apply or compare to a woman who focuses too much on her outward appearance?

- Discuss as a group what amount of time is appropriate to care for one's outward appearance.

- How is beauty fleeting? How is charm deceptive?

- What does this passage communicate is "most" important? Why is this not valued more in our world?

- How can we begin to put more attention on that which is the "most" important?

CLOSE OUT

- What's the common theme from all the Bible passages about appearance?

- Are you working extra hard on your appearance to hide something? Why?

- Are you dressing to attract someone or some kind of attention? Why?

- Are you spending equal time on your heart and character as you are to improve your appearance? Why or why not?

- How can we be a part of changing the culture that puts too much importance on appearance?

DO YOU NEED A FRIEND?

PRIMARY SCRIPTURES

Proverbs 17:17, 18:24, 12:26, 27:6

OBJECTIVES

- Identify the need for authentic friendships.
- Examine the different levels of friendships.
- Discuss the benefits to authentic friendships.

OVERVIEW

Since elementary school I have had more than 50 best friends. In elementary school, if my friend wanted to play a different game than I or made me mad, I began looking for a new "best" friend. I probably had a new best friend every week in those days! When I got to junior high things changed. I was lonely. I knew a lot of people and a lot of people knew me, but I didn't feel like people really knew who I was. In high school, I made a decision to be the kind of friend I was looking for. I decided to be trustworthy and to accept others for who they were instead of who I wanted them to be. In the process, I developed a friendship during my sophomore year that was unlike any I had ever had. Ten years later she was the maid of honor in my wedding.

High school taught me that I needed a few good friends rather than always seeking to be surrounded by a crowd. Crowds can be lonely so it's important to be known in a personal and meaningful way. I still knew lots of people in school, but I had one faithful friend I could trust and confide in. She knew everything about me and held me accountable. The world sends the message that more is better but God's Word says that "many companions" won't lead to anything good. But the outcome isn't the same for the person who has a friend that is closer than family. That is what my best friend from high school is, closer than family. We celebrate each other's joys and we cry when the other is in pain. What do you think your life would be like if you had a friend that was closer than family?

Friends come and friends go, but a true friend sticks by you like family (Proverbs 18:24 The Message).

LEADER'S STUDY
Proverbs 17:17, 18:24, 12:26, 27:6
Let's take a quick look at the scriptures used today in our Bible study.

Proverbs 17:17 – The writer communicates that no circumstance in this life should affect our love for our friends. Our love for others should not be based on what they can do for us.

Proverbs 18:24 – Finding a friend who will never leave you and love you just the way you are is better than having lots of "friends" who don't know the real you.

Proverbs 12:26 – The righteous are guided by things other than the world's values, so they are slow and wise in choosing friends, which helps them avoid being led astray.

Proverbs 27:6 – A good friend (someone who knows you deeply and loves you unconditionally) is a person you can trust to tell you the truth even when it hurts.

TO MAKE FRIENDS THAT LAST...
1. Be wise in choosing friends.
Friendship can't be rushed. We sometimes latch onto someone who may not be a good fit for us, so take your time and pick a friend that you know is someone you can trust.

TIP:
Talk about a "step" you took to make a friendship deeper and more authentic.

2. Be authentic in your friendships.
You can only be as close to your friends as you are willing to allow them. Sometimes it's important to ask if you are the reason you don't have close friends. Are you afraid to let anyone really know you?

3. Be willing to be held accountable.

When you trust others to tell you the truth, allow them to speak into your life. Another person is often better able to provide perspective to help us grow and develop. Truth can hurt, but it can also help us grow.

ADDITIONAL RESOURCES (OPTIONAL)

HABITS Tool - Back to Back card or Accountability Card
(Simply Youth Ministry Discipleship Resource - simplyyouthministry.com)
Allows girls to make a commitment with another girl or with the group for accountability.

Friendship Checklist

Have the students create a list of qualities they would like to have in a friend. Then use the list as self-examination of the type of friend they are to others.

DISCUSSION GUIDE
Open Up

- Can anyone remember their best friend from 2nd grade? Are you still friends with that person?

> **TIP:**
> Talk about how your friendships have changed as you've grown up, and how the "friend" things that seemed important in high school often aren't important as you get older.

- What does friendship mean to you? How important are friendships to you?

- What makes someone your friend? What kind of friend would you say you are?

Dig In

Transition into your study by talking about the benefits of genuine friendship (accountability, safety, a place you can be yourself). Share a story or an example of a significant friendship in your life. The Bible points out the need for and the benefits of deep, authentic friendships. Unfortunately, many of us avoid that level of friendship because we are uncomfortable with another knowing so much about us. Today we'll explore what defines an authentic friendship and what steps to take in order to add them to your life.

Read and discuss Proverbs 17:17, 18:24, 12:26, 27:6

- Do you have a friend that loves you at all times? What does that kind of love feel like? Do you have a friend that is closer than family?

- What is the difference between a shallow friendship and an authentic friendship?

- Why do you think that many friendships lead to ruin? Have you seen this happen at your school or in your circle of friendships?

- Why is the wise person cautious in friendships? What does the scripture say will happen if you are unwise?

- What are wounds from a friend? And how can they be trusted?

- What does it say about a friendship that you can trust wounds from that person?

CLOSE OUT

- What's the common theme from all the Bible passages about friendship?

- Why do you think friendships are so important to us? Do you think we avoid deep friendships? Why?

- How can you be a better friend to those around you?

- Are you allowing those close to you to really know you? Are you allowing them to speak into your life?

- What steps can we take to move our friendship from shallow to real, creating a place of trust and accountability?

WHO'S RUNNING FOR PRESIDENT?

PRIMARY SCRIPTURES

Proverbs 14:20, 24:23, 28:21-23

OBJECTIVES

- Openly and honestly explore the world of girl politics.
- Examine the reasons why girls create their own "rules" and "systems."
- Discuss the value in eliminating the lies that girls perpetuate.

OVERVIEW

There is no denying that teenage girls can be MEAN! In fact, in 2005 a movie based on the book *Queen Bees and Wannabes* focused on this subject. In all my time with working with teenage girls I have been amazed by the underlying code of conduct girls live by. It's a teenage girl "caste system" almost as clear as the one in India. I can't help but think the devil is responsible for the damage this type of system creates in the lives of teenage girls.

TIP:
You might need to do a little online research to understand or explain the details of a "caste system."

There seem to be some unspoken rules of girl politics. Certain girls can hang out in particular groups, and no one questions it. Unwritten rules guiding behavior are everywhere—we can't escape them. I find myself asking, "Who makes the rules?" and "Why?" Why are we quick to adhere to modern rules guiding what clothes to wear or music to listen to or people to spend time with? These rules of favoritism not only damage our view of others but also our view of ourselves. But there is good news! God has a new set of rules that communicate love and value.

Since God created us and loves us He wants us to know every person has value, whether rich or poor, skinny or fat, smart or average, well dressed or not.

These also are sayings of the wise: To show partiality in judging is not good (Proverbs 24:23).

LEADER'S STUDY
Proverbs 14:20, 24:23, 28:21-23
Let's take a quick look at the scriptures used today in our Bible study.

Proverbs 14:20 - Judging others has been going on since the beginning of time. In the world of girl politics, it's always about what other people can do for you. Relationships are based on self-interest.

Proverbs 24:23 – Showing partiality is not good! Treating people differently based on what you perceive about them is not the way of wisdom and God.

Proverbs 28:21-23 - The writer is telling us how little it takes for one to be deceived.

HOW TO SURVIVE GIRL POLITICS.
1. Start by admitting that it exists.
Sometimes the main problem with girl politics is that everyone knows it's going on but is afraid to admit it. What would happen if we started to acknowledge this underlying system and decided that we weren't going to be a part of it? I think you would be amazed by the new friends you would make.

2. Don't show partiality.
Do you think you treat all people with the same respect and civility? If you don't, ask yourself what is it that causes you to show favoritism to some while not to others? This sometimes requires changing your filters (the standards by which you look at people) and asking God to give you the ability to treat all people the same.

3. Watch your words.
Who are you trying to please with your words? Are you trying to gain approval or status from others? If so, you may find yourself giving in to the politics and trying to sell yourself as something you really aren't. It could be as simple as using bad language to fit in or making up things to be accepted. Often we try to impress the same people who are trying to impress us. If you don't believe me, start by examining your MySpace page!

DISCUSSION GUIDE
Open Up

TIP:
Consider using a clip
from the movie.

- Did you see the movie *Mean Girls*? Do you think the movie painted an accurate picture of the teenage years?

- When you hear the words "girl politics," what do you think?

- What are some of the rules of girl world?

- What kind of damage do you think these rules and systems have on you and other girls around you?

DIG IN

Transition into your study by honestly exposing the truth about girl politics (i.e., we know it exists; girls set up standards that other girls have to live by in order to be accepted or to fit in). Share a story from your teenage years about how "girl politics" affected you. Girl politics boils down to showing partiality and favoritism in a world that so desperately needs a healthy view of itself. These politics existed thousands of years ago, yet the Bible clearly explains that they aren't good. Today we are going to talk about the pitfalls of girl politics and how we can be a part of changing the system.

Read and discuss Proverbs 14:20, 24:23, 28:21-23
- Why are the poor shunned? Why do the rich have friends?

- What does Proverbs 14:20 communicate about the depths of these friendships?

- Define partiality. How does it exist in the world of teenage girls?

TIP:
Talk about how
you can help each
other with any
consequences at
breaking the "rules"
of girl politics.

- Why do you think the writer of Proverbs said partiality is bad? Do you agree or disagree?

- In the world of girl politics, what would "a piece of bread" be? In other words, what are girls willing to compromise their views for? Acceptance? Approval?

- Do you think people still use their wealth and words to gain a certain status? Share why you agree or disagree with doing that.

CLOSE OUT
- What's the common theme from all the Bible passages about how to treat people? How do they contradict what is happening in the midst of girl politics?

- What are the downfalls of girl politics? How are they affecting you and those around you?

- Do you think that you have gotten caught up in the games girls play? Or do you think you have been a victim of the game?

- How do you think you can be part of changing the way girls treat other girls? Are you willing to do those things?

- What's one action you can take in the next week to begin breaking down the walls that girl politics have created?

CAN YOU KEEP A SECRET?

PRIMARY SCRIPTURES

Proverbs 16:28, 26:20, 11:13, 20:19

OBJECTIVES

- Identify the source of gossip in girls' lives.
- Contrast the outcomes of gossip and keeping secrets.
- Discuss the disappointment that results from gossip.

OVERVIEW

It's with great disappointment that I admit that all my life I have battled gossip. In fact, I wonder if I came out of my mother's womb talking about other people! I don't like the results of gossip, but I can't seem to help myself. I do it even when I don't want to—it just happens. Get me in a group of my girlfriends and ask me about somebody—anybody—and I'll tell you all that I know about them.

Just this last week in my small group, one of the girls mentioned that one of her goals for the year is to stop talking about other people. Why does every girl battle taming the tongue? Even when we are innocently trying to share "prayer requests" it somehow crosses the line of sharing needs to sharing secrets. Not only does this seem to be a modern day problem but if you read scriptures in both the Old and New Testament, you'll find that it was occurring in the early church, too.

TIP:

Consider sharing a personal example as the creator or the victim of gossip.

Not only can I tell you about my problem with sharing gossip but I could spend all day writing stories of how gossip has hurt me, whether it was a secret shared by someone I trusted or an untrue story about me spread around the school or workplace. So many people, not just me, have been hurt or damaged by gossip and its power to destroy.

How do we help young women overcome this "legendary" problem? Is there really help for it? As we examine scripture, we'll discover the root of gossip and its destructive power. But at the same time we'll find hope for overcoming this habit and find hope for our relationships. Let's dive in together and discover how to keep a secret!

A gossip betrays a confidence, but a trustworthy man keeps a secret (Proverbs 11:13).

LEADER'S STUDY
Proverbs 16:28, 26:20, 11:13, 20:19
Let's take a quick look at the scriptures used today in our Bible study.

Proverbs 16:28 – The passage addresses the character of the person spreading words that cause dissension. Girls need to figure out the character within them that causes them to spread rumors. Insecurity turns girls into hurtful people who will at times do or say things to make them feel better about themselves. The passage also addresses the fact that gossip has the power to separate close friends. The very relationships that girls long for are destroyed by their own insecurities.

Proverbs 26:20 – What happens to an argument between girls when gossip gets added to the mix? It grows and never ends. Gossip is never the solution. In fact Matthew 5:23-26 provides the proper way to handle conflict by going directly to the person and working it out.

Proverbs 11:13 – The scripture tells us that gossip is not trustworthy so be careful who you trust with a secret. We all have learned who is worthy of hearing our secrets and who can't be trusted based on our past experiences.

Proverbs 20:19 – The scripture provides advice about how to choose friends. Don't choose one who can't keep a secret because they talk too much. The quality of the friendship will be determined by how much the person talks. Girls usually don't think about that when picking friends.

LEARNING TO KEEP A SECRET

1. Realize the root of gossip is about your character.

The very act of gossip goes deeper than the surface; it describes the heart of the person sharing it. When we share secrets that friends have confided in us or talk about what we "heard" it is often because we know attention will be diverted away from us. We need to examine our hearts before anyone will be able to keep a secret.

2. Understand that gossip always leads to pain.

Gossip never…EVER…leads to good, even when it comes in the form of a prayer request! Whether the pain is minor or deep, gossip hurts those it's about and those who are spreading it.

3. Acknowledge that great friendships can come out of making a commitment to stay gossip-free.

Finding a friend you trust is one of the best joys in life. We all need close friends, and close friendships can only develop in the safety of knowing that what you share in private will stay in private.

ADDITIONAL RESOURCES (OPTIONAL)

Gossip Free Commitment Cards

Wallet-size card with the following pledge and a place for their signature:
I, INSERT NAME, make a commitment to use my words for good instead of causing pain. I recognize my words have power and I will use them to bless rather than hurt. I will do what it takes to be a trustworthy woman of God.
SIGNATURE SPOT

Gossip Magazine Challenge

Supply the group with several gossip magazines (*People, USWeekly,* etc.) and ask the girls to identify articles that are filled with gossip and those that are non-gossip articles. Help the girls identify the difference between telling a story and sharing juicy gossip.

Create a Gossip Checklist

A ¼ sheet card with questions to help identify when our words turn to gossip:
- Is the story and/or information I am about to share true?
- Would I share the story and/or information if all the people it was about were here right now?
- Would I want this story and/or information shared about me to others without me around?

- Is the story and/or information helpful to someone?
- Will this story and/or information help resolve conflict between friends?
- Is this story and/or information helping me become a trustworthy person?

If you answered NO to any of these questions, it would be better to keep what you were about to say to yourself!

DISCUSSION GUIDE
Open Up
- What current celebrity stories is everyone talking about? Would you define this as gossip? Why or why not?

- Can anyone define the word "gossip"?

- What kind of effects has gossip had on your relationships?

TIP:
If your youth group has faced recent gossip issues, this lesson can be a chance to take a healing step.

DIG IN
Transition into your study by explaining the definition of gossip (spreading rumors or talk of a personal, sensational, or intimate nature). This would be a great place to share a personal story of how gossip may have hurt you when you were a student. Depending on the size of your group you could ask students to share similar stories. The scriptures point out the negative effects that gossip can have on relationships and examine the character of a person whose mouth is filled with gossip. Today we'll explore why we gossip and work together to determine ways that we can be trustworthy and confident friends.

Read and discuss Proverbs 16:28, 26:20, 11:13, 20:19
- Have you ever experienced the separation that gossip brings to your friendships? Are these scriptures accurate about the pitfalls of gossip to your friendships?

- Why do you think gossip keeps the fire of conflict going?

- What does confidence in a person mean? How does a person get confidence in you? How can a person lose confidence?

- Is spreading gossip worth losing the confidence of a close friend? If not, why do you think that we keep doing it? Does it say anything about how we value our friendships?

- All the scriptures refer to the character of a gossip and the character of someone who keeps a secret. What's the difference between the two types?

- How does someone become a trustworthy person?

- How can we learn to control our tongue?

CLOSE OUT
- What's the common theme from all the Bible passages about gossip?

- Why do you think girls gossip? What does gossip say about the person spreading it?

- What are steps we can take to control our tongues?

- If we seek to eliminate gossip from our lives, what will happen to our friendships and to our self-worth?

MIRROR, MIRROR ON THE WALL

OBJECTIVES

- Identify the messages that the world sends about our worth.
- Examine the reasons why we believe the world's messages.
- Discuss what we see when we look inside ourselves.

PRIMARY SCRIPTURES
Proverbs 19:8, 20:27, 27:19

OVERVIEW

Sometimes I get a glimpse of myself in the mirror and it is almost like I forgot what I looked like. Instead of thinking of all the many beautiful parts of my face and body, I focus on the few parts I dislike about myself. I forget about my heart, character, and love for God and think about my nose, ears, and boney elbows. I can't help but see myself as nothing but a body. And when that happens, I sink into a place of low self-worth. I want to like myself and believe that I am important and valuable, but in order to do that I must look deeper than what the mirror reveals.

TIP:
Consider a movie clip from *Snow White* or the *Shrek* movies, with the magic mirror.

This is not just another lesson on what we look like but rather a deeper look at how we feel about ourselves inside and out. We already know that the world sends messages about our worth but what messages do we send ourselves? If we can identify the lies that the world sends we will be able to identify they are not true. What happens when we start to see ourselves based on what's within our heart and our souls instead of what's staring back at us in the mirror?

As water reflects the face, so one's life reflects the heart (Proverbs 27:19 TNIV).

LEADER'S STUDY
Proverbs 19:8, 20:27, 27:19

Let's take a quick look at the scriptures used today in our Bible study.

Proverbs 19:8 – Those who seek wisdom give themselves the best chance to succeed in life. If you love yourself, you'll search for the right stuff. It doesn't say anything negative about loving yourself; in fact it says it's the right thing to do. What would happen in the lives of teenage girls if they loved their own souls?

Proverbs 20:27 – The passage points us to a deeper us, the spirit within us. When God looks at us, He doesn't see our body, He sees our spirit. In fact, He searches our spirit to find the real us. God cares for us in a more intimate sense, so we should care about ourselves in that same way.

Proverbs 27:19 – Our hearts reflect who we really are just like water reflects a face. Who we really are is about our heart, not our looks or anything else. The message from the world couldn't be more opposite than that. What determines our value is not our bodies but our heart. What's inside your heart?

HOW TO KNOW HOW YOU FEEL ABOUT YOURSELF...

1. Start describing yourself by your character instead of your appearance.
The next time someone asks you to describe yourself, reveal elements of your character and personality rather than physical attributes. Practice looking in the mirror and focus on what's inside your body.

2. Take extra time to examine what's in your heart.
If we are more than our bodies, we need to start taking time to see what is hidden in our hearts. We need to discover the things that are good and help them grow stronger. We also need to find the things that need work and start spending time making improvements to the condition of our hearts. We need to love our souls!

3. Reflect what's in your heart for others to see.
Carry yourself confidently and walk with your head lifted high. Now that you know the good inside your heart, make sure you reflect it to others. You'll be surprised how people will respond to the new confidence that you have found within yourself.

DISCUSSION GUIDE
Open Up

- In society today, what makes a woman valuable?

- How do you think those "values" affect people?

- On average, do you think that girls your age feel bad, good, or in the middle about themselves? What are these feelings usually based on (looks, skills, friends, etc.)?

Dig In

Transition into your study by explaining that for too long we have let the world determine the value of our image. The Bible teaches that we are made up of more than our body or the superficial things that we can be judged by. In fact, we are soul and spirit. That means the best indication of who we really are comes from inside our hearts, not our bodies. Our "image" is more about what's reflected for all to see from our hearts, not our outward appearance. Today we'll explore who we really are by exposing the values of the world and by examining God's Word for the truth on what really makes us...well...us!

> **TIP:**
> See if you can borrow a "crazy" mirror like the ones in a fun house that distort reality.

Read and discuss Proverbs 19:8, 20:27, 27:19

- What does it mean to love your own soul? According to the Bible, what actions should we take if we really love ourselves?

- What do you typically think when someone says they love themselves?

- What does God search? Explain what you think our spirit is.

- Has anyone ever judged you on your soul/spirit? How is that different from how the world normally judges? If it's happened, how did it make you feel?

- According to Proverbs 27:19, what reflects who a person is? Does that agree or disagree with the messages the world sends us?

- If a heart is who a person is, why do you think society puts such little emphasis on it?

CLOSE OUT

- What's the common theme from all the Bible passages about what makes up our image?

- Do the things you choose to do communicate that you love yourself or dislike yourself?

- What is the condition of your spirit? If God is searching it, what does He find?

- What is your heart reflecting about the person you really are? How is that different than what others say or think about you?

- Before today, did you base your image on anything other than superficial elements? If so, how does today's lesson change your view of your image?

KINDNESS - IT CAN MAKE ALL THE DIFFERENCE

PRIMARY SCRIPTURES

Proverbs 10:12, 10:21, 11:16, 12:25

OBJECTIVES

- Define kindness and how it affects others.
- Explore what could happen in the world when one person chooses to show kindness.
- Discuss practical ways to be kind to others.

OVERVIEW

Before I realized what I had done the words were out of my mouth, and I knew immediately that I made a wrong choice. I am not sure why I said those hurtful words, but I do know they came out much too easily. In our world today, tearing people down with our words is considered normal while building others up is not.

TIP:
Talk about random acts of kindness; encourage the girls to perform these kinds of acts.

Sometimes I like to dream about what my life would be like if I were the kindest person on earth. Would I be like Oprah? Or Mother Teresa? What kind of difference would I make? And sometimes I like to dream about what the world would look like if we all decided to be kind instead of hurtful. I know there are many things I could do to make a difference and I can only imagine what the world would be like if everyone decided to show kindness. The reality is that we don't need to be like Oprah or Mother Teresa but we can show kindness in simple, everyday ways with our words and our actions. And not only would the world benefit but showing kindness to others would benefit us, too!

A kindhearted woman gains respect (Proverbs 11:16).

LEADER'S STUDY
Proverbs 10:12, 10:21, 11:16, 12:25
Let's take a quick look at the scriptures used today in our Bible study.

Proverbs 10:12 – The author of this passage points out the benefits of loving others versus the consequences of not loving others.

Proverbs 10:21 – Our very words can nourish and cultivate life for another person if we choose to use them for good rather than harm. This verse reminds us that if we use judgment before we speak we can help others instead of hurt them.

Proverbs 11:16 – A woman with a kind heart gains respect. Even in a world that has made it easy to be cruel, kindness still leads to the respect we crave.

Proverbs 12:25 – The worries of this world can weigh a person down but just one kind word can cheer a person up. One kind word can make all the difference.

HOW AND WHERE TO SHOW KINDNESS
How?
1. With your words.
Whoever came up with the saying "sticks and stones can break your bones but words will never hurt you" was a liar. Words have power. We can change someone's life by using words that build up instead of tear down.

2. With your actions.
Kindness is so much more than words. It's about seeing those in need around us and responding in any way that we can, whether it's a helping hand or giving money to someone in greater need than ourselves.

Where?
1. In your home.
Sometimes we forget the very first place to show kindness is in our own homes, to our parents or our siblings. Sometimes this is the hardest place to start.

2. In your school.
When was the last time you showed kindness to another student or a teacher at school? What would your school look like if people continuously showed kindness?

3. In your community.

Is there a single parent in your neighborhood who could use a helping hand with child care or lawn work? Imagine the difference you could make in their day, week, month or year.

4. In your world.

Statistically speaking, you are already more fortunate than most of the rest of the world. You can decide to use all that you have been given by helping others who are less fortunate than you.

ADDITIONAL RESOURCES (OPTIONAL)

A "Kind" Memory – Give each girl a ½ sheet of paper to write out one memory they have of another person showing them kindness. Make sure they include the impact the act of kindness had on them. If time permits, have the girls share their memories.

Kindness Commitment – A small commitment card with a place to sign their name: "I will use my words to build others up. I will serve others when it's not convenient for me. I will try new ways of showing kindness to others in the next 30 days." (It only takes 30 days to develop a habit).

TIP:
We all know the differences between Simon's style and Paula's style. For all her weaknesses, Paula does seem to be the more "encouraging" judge.

DISCUSSION GUIDE
Open Up

- Would you rather have Simon Cowell judge your singing or Paula Abdul? Why?

- Can anyone define kindness? How does a kind person act?

- Can you think of a time that someone showed you kindness? How did it make you feel?

Dig In

Transition into your study by explaining the importance of showing kindness in a hurting world and how simple acts of kindness can make a difference. Share a story of how someone's kindness impacted you. The Bible teaches that kindness can make a world of difference in the lives of people who are broken and hurt. If we take a moment to think about how we can use our words and our actions to encourage others, we might be surprised to find out how much of an impact that it can make on others and ourselves. Today we'll explore the results of showing kindness to others.

Read and discuss Proverbs 10:12, 10:21, 11:16, 12:25

- According to Proverbs 10:12, what does love in action do? Do you think love is that powerful?

- How can righteous lips nourish people? Can you think of a time that someone's words nourished you?

- Define kindhearted. Do you know any women who you would define as kindhearted?

- Is the respect of others something that you value? Do you agree that kindness is the way to earn it from others?

- What weighs a person down? Have you ever felt weighed down by the worries of the world?

- If you have felt weighed down by the world's worries, do you think that a kind word could change your outlook on life?

- Do you think your words can change someone else's outlook on life? If so, what does that say about the power of your words?

TIP:
Take a few minutes to have each girl share something positive about another girl in the group.

CLOSE OUT
- What's the common theme from all the Bible passages about kindness?

- Do you think most people would describe you as kind? If not, how would they describe you? What would you like to change in your life?

- What type of difference do you think words or acts of kindness could make in the lives around you?

- Is there a specific person in your life that you know you could be more kind to? What are some things you can do this week to change the way you treat them?

IS PURE BETTER?

OBJECTIVES

- Identify God's plan for our purity.
- Examine why girls choose not to live a life of purity.
- Discuss the benefits of maintaining a pure heart and mind.

OVERVIEW

Recently, I was on an airplane filled with over 30 teenage girls who were returning from a cheer competition. I sat next to two of the girls who pulled out a women's magazine and began reading an article out loud about how to please a man in bed. One of the girls was only fifteen years old—fifteen and reading an article in an adult magazine about how to sexually please a man.

Purity can often be a misunderstood word. While some people may consider purity to be a foolish thing to pursue, God calls us to be pure. And He doesn't just call us to be pure physically but in our mind, heart, and body. God wants us to stay away from the lies and contamination of the world's messages and instead to choose purity.

The LORD detests the thoughts of the wicked, but those of the pure are pleasing to him (Proverbs 15:26).

LEADER'S STUDY
Proverbs 5:6, 20:11, 15:26

Let's take a quick look at the scriptures used today in our Bible study:

Proverbs 5:6 – The she in this passage is the adulteress woman, one who hasn't chosen purity. The scripture says that she doesn't even give thought to it but instead staggers through life blindly and destructively. Making a commitment to choose God's way for purity demands intentionality that begins in our heart and mind.

Proverbs 15:26 – This is a strong verse: God detests the "thoughts" of the wicked. It doesn't say anything about God detesting people but rather their impure thoughts. Purity is so important to God that it stirs up an emotion within the creator of the world. The flipside to this emotion is that those who make a commitment to purity please God.

Proverbs 20:11 – The character of a person is known by others and you are never too young to be known for your purity. Purity is recognizable by others because it is lived out in action. Purity starts with a commitment that is lived out in front of others.

WHY PURITY IS MORE THAN NOT HAVING SEX:

1. It's about purity of your heart.
Every commitment begins in the heart and it has to be bigger than saying "I won't have sex," because purity is about resisting the world's way of doing things. The challenge is to make a commitment that guards your heart, mind, and body from anything that would contaminate you with the sin from the world.

2. It's about purity of your mind.
A lot of us feel good about ourselves because we aren't out having sex, but the thoughts and things that we put into our minds are just as damaging. Think about the magazines that you read, the movies you watch, and the songs you listen to. What messages are they sending? It's not about avoiding "the world" but it's about making daily decisions that help maintain the purity of your mind versus allowing it to be contaminated.

3. It's about purity of your motives.
When your heart and mind are pure the results are actions motivated by purity. But when you begin to let yourself be swayed by the world's messages, you find yourself making decisions or leading others to make decisions out of wrong

motives. Wrong motives are those that are about only fulfilling your own selfish desires, such as instant gratification or approval from others, or whatever they may be.

DISCUSSION GUIDE
Open Up
- What are words that you associate with purity?

- Would you say that typically people who have chosen to abstain from certain conversations or activities are considered pure, naïve or sheltered?

- Do you think purity is an important value today among teenage girls? Why?

TIP:
When revealing these kinds of weaknesses, emphasize God's grace and forgiveness. Don't get caught up in too many of the "dirty" details, or else it can feel like you're glorifying the sin.

DIG IN
Transition into your study by discussing the definition of purity (keeping oneself from being contaminated or diluted by the sin and the world's messages). If it's appropriate, share a story of how your commitment or lack of commitment to purity has affected your life. The scriptures point out the value of needing to keep oneself pure for both honoring God and for living a life free of regrets and disappointments. Today we'll explore why purity is so important and what we can do to achieve it in our lives.

Read and discuss Proverbs 5:6, 15:26, 20:11
- Look at Proverbs 5:6. Who is the "she" in this passage?

- What doesn't she give any thought to? Describe the path that follows her decision.

- Do you agree that making the right decision requires effort and work?

- What are people defined by? Is that the same today?

- When the author says that even a child is known by her actions, what principle is conveyed?

- Describe the emotions of God that are expressed in this passage. What does it say about God and purity?

- What about "the pure" are pleasing to God?

TIP:
This is a great lesson for talking about the role and value of accountability partners.

CLOSE OUT
- What's the common theme from all the Bible passages about purity?

- Purity starts with making a commitment. Why do you think it's important to make a commitment?

- In this world do you think that it's hard to maintain purity of heart and mind? What's the difference between keeping your heart and mind pure?

- What are some of the main reasons people struggle with keeping their commitment to purity?

- What steps can you take to maintain your purity in today's world?

THE BIG DEAL ABOUT SEX

PRIMARY SCRIPTURES

Proverbs 16:25, 30:18-19, 30:20

OBJECTIVES

- Identify what the world says about sex and determine if it's true.
- Explore the differences between girls and guys.
- Examine the truth from God's Word about sex.

OVERVIEW

Most teenage girls learn everything they know about sex from the TV, movies, music or popular magazines. This is scary considering most, if not all, of those messages are inaccurate. The world makes sex look less complicated than it really is, creating a false illusion about the consequences or lack thereof of sex. And the media fail to communicate how differently guys and girls view sex, which makes for confusing messages in their relationships.

As I was growing up, the church's only message about sex was "don't do it!" But over the last few years the church has done a better job speaking about God's original design for sex. Sex isn't bad when it's enjoyed in the context of marriage, the way God intended it. This lesson isn't about how bad sex is but about the lies and traps the world sends regarding giving in to our own sexual desires. Living by God's plan, ultimately, is what's best for us.

There is a way that seems right to a man, but in the end it leads to death (Proverbs 16:25).

LEADER'S STUDY
Proverbs 16:25, 30:18-19, 30:20

Let's take a quick look at the scriptures used today in our Bible study.
All of these scriptures counter the messages sent by the world about sex.

Proverbs 16:25 – When the consequences of our decisions are never talked about we often think the choices that we are making are right. Not thinking about whether the messages the world sends about sex are true and examining the consequences of those messages can lead one to think that acting on your own desires is not only right but that it won't cause any harm.

Proverbs 30:18-19 – This is a funny passage about the writer's observations of four things that amaze him. The humor in this passage is that all these different elements of nature are overwhelming to the author, but his final observation revolves around the way a man is with a woman. This is one clear passage about the difference between guys and girls—notice the author didn't say the way a woman is with a man. Even the Bible recognizes there are differences between guys and girls.

Proverbs 30:20 – The writer addresses the attitude of the adulteress that makes choices without regard to consequences. Our society has told us to do whatever feels good and to not feel regret for our bad decisions. "If it feels goods…" "Whatever makes you happy…" are messages that don't consider the future or God's plans for our life.

STEPS TO TAKE:
1. Acknowledge that the world is misleading us.
We have to acknowledge that the messages we receive from the world about sex and relationships are not true. Although they make for great story lines, the media glamorize the romantic elements of love and sex without touching the issues of commitment and intimacy. A recent study showed that over 75% of girls who had sex before they were married rated it as disappointing—simply because they bought the world's lies and were surprised to find that love and sex are completely different than what they were told.

2. Discover the truth from God's Word.
God's designs for our relationships are perfect! I remember being young and doubting I could trust God's plan, afraid I would never experience love for myself. But the more I watched my friends make decisions based on the world's message and the pain that resulted, the more convinced I became that God's Word was the truth. By following God's plan I spared myself and my husband a

lot of pain and disappointment. Plus I found that God's Word provided me a lot of practical insight into making my relationships work since He was the one who created us as man and woman.

3. Make decisions based on all the facts.

Each person needs to discover all the facts and make decisions about their plan of action. Relationships and sex are not something that you can remain undecided on as no decision is a slow progression to the wrong decision. Discover God's plan for you and make a commitment to live it out in all areas of your relationships.

ADDITIONAL RESOURCES (OPTIONAL)

Find a woman in your church that would we billing to share (in a healthy way) her story of bad decisions that she made sexually and the consequences she faced from her decisions.

Bring in a guest speaker from an organization like the Crisis Pregnancy Center to talk about some of her experiences and some of the pressures teenage girls face sexually.

TIP:
See if you can create a list of TV shows with good, positive messages about sex. It's tough!

DISCUSSION GUIDE
Open Up
- What is your favorite TV show?

- Does that show communicate any messages regarding sex? If so, what messages are sent?

- Do you think guys and girls think the same about dating and sex? If not, how do our views differ?

DIG IN

Transition into your study by explaining how relationships and sex are misunderstood in our world today. God created sex to be enjoyed in the context of marriage as something special and sacred between two people. But the world has turned sex into something that is purely entertainment with no lasting effects. This leads many people to make decisions about sex that produce a lifetime of shallow relationships and disappointment. Today we'll explore what the Bible says about sex and decision making.

Read and discuss Proverbs 16:25, 30:18-19, 30:20

- According to the world, what seems "right" about the values of dating and sex?

- What does the writer say will happen to those who follow the values of the world?

- What is the way of the adulteress woman? What do you think it means?

- Does the world often talk about the consequences of the decisions we make regarding dating and sex? (Aside form STDs and pregnancy)

- What are the four things that amaze the author? Do you think anything is funny about this passage?

- What does this verse communicate about the difference between guys and girls?

- Why do you think the author didn't state this the other way around? Do you agree or disagree with the author?

TIP:
Each family is different, but encourage your girls to talk with their parents about the topics you've discussed in this lesson.

CLOSE OUT

- What's the common theme from all the Bible passages about the decisions we make involving dating and sex?

- Do you think it's true that the messages sent by the world regarding sex are false? Why or why not?

- Do you think we live in a society that rarely thinks about the consequences of their choices? Have you experienced any consequences of making decisions based on the world's way? Are you open to sharing?

- Do you think God's design is best? If so, what steps can you take to follow it?

FINDING YOUR WORTH

PRIMARY SCRIPTURES

Proverbs 4:23, 21:3, 21:21

OBJECTIVES

- Explore how God views us.
- Examine the differences between God's view and our view of ourselves.
- Discuss the power that this truth can give us.

OVERVIEW

Can you remember the last compliment that you got about your appearance? How about the last compliment about your heart? My 11th grade science teacher said something to me that I'll never forget, "You really care about others and you can see it in how you treat people." I was amazed someone noticed me for more than my looks or my loud laugh—they noticed my heart. That compliment stuck with me for a long time and motivated me to make the right decisions.

What I liked so much about that compliment was that it was not only about something that was natural for me but it spoke about the goodness within me. That compliment helped me to start seeing my heart the way God saw it and when that happened, my whole perspective of myself began to change.

I realized I was God's child and my desire to make good choices came from Him. I can't tell you how my self-esteem improved when I understood that God wasn't looking at me with disappointment but with awe. It completely changed how I viewed myself. As women we spend so much time looking for our faults that we rarely take time to see all the good within us. And this good has nothing to do with the way we perform or the things we do but it's solely about our heart.

Our heart has value. The Bible says our heart is the most important part of who we are. Christ died to redeem our heart—it's just that important.

Above all else, guard your heart, for it is the wellspring of life (Proverbs 4:23).

LEADER'S STUDY
Proverbs 4:23, 21:3, 21:21
Let's take a quick look at the scriptures used today in our Bible study.

TIP:
Send an encouraging note to your girls' parents, reminding them that they can still speak positive words into the hearts of their girls.

Proverbs 4:23 – The writer suggests that more than anything your heart is important. Guard it for it is where all of your life comes from. Not just physically but spiritually it is your most valuable element.

Proverbs 21:3 –God wants us to have a heart that seeks what is right far more than He wants us to sacrifice for Him. If you tear away all the other stuff that we try to fill our hearts with, you will find a heart that longs for righteousness and justice.

Proverbs 21:21 – When you pursue righteousness and love from your heart you find real life. Both righteousness and love are the very things that your heart was created for.

WHY YOUR HEART IS VALUABLE...
1. It's your source of life.
Not only does your heart keep you alive physically but it is the very source of who God made you to be. What does that mean? It means that your ability to feel, love, and do good things comes directly from your heart.

2. It was created for good.
When God created us, everything about us was good. Even though sin later entered the world and affected every person alive, God can heal us and allow us to live the way He always intended.

3. It has great potential.

Sure God created us to do good, but a healthy heart has the potential to not only motivate us but also inspire others to know that God loves them and offers hope to them. Strengthening our self-esteem enables us to believe all God says about us.

DISCUSSION GUIDE

Open Up

- Share a funny story from your childhood when you got in trouble for something and you didn't understand what you did wrong.

- Share a story from your childhood when you won an award or made a special achievement.

- On a whole, do you think people are naturally good or bad?

Dig In

Transition into the study by explaining that most of our lives we have been sent messages that we aren't good. While we are born with a sinful nature, and we too often naturally choose what's wrong, it's also true that from the beginning of creation our hearts have had a longing and desire to know God and be good. When God looks at our heart, He sees good! Not only is this clear in Proverbs but it's clear throughout the Bible. Today we'll explore the issues of the heart and why the condition of our heart gives us value rather than the things we do.

Read and discuss Proverbs 4:23, 21:3, 21:21

- What does the word wellspring mean? Why do you think the writer refers to the heart as the wellspring?

TIP:
Your girls probably care about their physical heart condition. A spiritually healthy heart takes effort, too!

- Why do you think it's important to guard our heart?

- Does the writer say anything needs to be done in order for our heart to be a wellspring? What does that say about the value of our hearts?

- What's more important than sacrifice?

- Do you think that doing what is right and just comes naturally to people? Why or why not?

- Where does the source of our love come from? Do you think that we naturally pursue love?

- What will one find by pursuing love and righteousness?

CLOSE OUT

- What's the common theme from all the Bible passages about our heart?

- Most of our lives we are sent messages that we aren't good. Do you think that is true?

- If our heart is so important, not because of anything we have done, what does that communicate about our value?

- How can understanding our heart's importance and value affect our self-image?

HE'LL TAKE YOU...WHERE?

PRIMARY SCRIPTURES

Proverbs 3:5-6, 16:3, 16:9

OBJECTIVES

- Identify the greatest place to find our self-worth.
- Explore all that God has for us and how that speaks to our worth.
- Discuss the potential of where God can take us.

OVERVIEW

I love how God's Word is filled with so many amazing examples of women who had such confidence in God that they did things and went places they never would have done on their own. Esther, Deborah, Jael, Mary, Lydia...the list goes on and on. I wonder if these women ever questioned their worth or value, however. Did they compare themselves to the women around them? I don't want to assume they didn't have doubts about themselves or moments when they questioned their value, but I can't help but think they were so radically consumed with what God had in store for them that they didn't have time to doubt who they were as they journeyed with God.

TIP:

For extra depth or for group follow-up, have the girls read about these and other strong women in the Bible.

Even though God always has a plan for me, I can't always see it. I have days where I get a glimpse of God's amazing plans for me and I am blown away by the fact that he would think of including me. He must really like me! And He must think I am good for something.

Imagine if all of us could understand that the Creator of the universe, the Maker of all things, is concerned about our steps and has designed great plans for us. I think if we could get some understanding of this, we would be overwhelmed by our self-worth. We would finally see the potential of our life and that potential would fill within us our greatest need for value and worth.

Commit to the LORD whatever you do, and your plans will succeed (Proverbs 16:3).

LEADER'S STUDY
Proverbs 3:5-6, 16:3, 16:9
Let's take a quick look at the scriptures used today in our Bible study.

Proverbs 3:5-6 – When you completely trust in God and His plans for you, He will be faithful to meet you and guide you. To know that we just simply have to lean on God because He values us so much, we can be confident that He'll do the rest.

Proverbs 16:3 – God cares so deeply for us that He asks us to simply rely on Him and let Him carry the burden of the task. He wants us to succeed and His plans and hopes for us include good things. Even in the midst of hard times, knowing that God's ultimate plan for us is good allows us to have deep confidence in Him, ourselves, and our futures.

TIP:
Remember, part of your role as a small group leader is to instill value in their lives, too. It's a special opportunity!

Proverbs 16:9 – The Creator of the universe cares about each of our steps. Not only does He care but He is deeply involved in each one. So many people will try and tell us that God is far away and uninvolved in our lives but the scriptures tell us that God is near, that He cares and is behind each of our steps.

WHAT'S GOD'S PLAN FOR MY LIFE HAVE TO DO WITH MY VALUE?
1. I am important enough to matter to the Creator.
What happens to you today matters to God. He cares about your feelings and your worries. He is intimately involved in your life and yet He's keeping the whole universe in action. I am not sure all that it takes to run the world (check out Job 38) but I can imagine it's a busy job. Despite that we are important enough to God that He takes time to care about us and the details of our lives. Think about this: you are God's child, the daughter of a King—a princess!